Giants of the Earth

Mitch Kehetian

PublishAmerica
Baltimore

© 2009 by Mitch Kehetian.
All rights reserved. No part of this book may be reproduced, stored in a retrieval system or transmitted in any form or by any means without the prior written permission of the publishers, except by a reviewer who may quote brief passages in a review to be printed in a newspaper, magazine or journal.

First printing

PublishAmerica has allowed this work to remain exactly as the author intended, verbatim, without editorial input.

ISBN: 978-1-61582-000-9 (softcover)
ISBN: 978-1-4489-9553-0 (hardcover)
PUBLISHED BY PUBLISHAMERICA, LLLP
www.publishamerica.com
Baltimore

Printed in the United States of America

It was genocide—
Mitch Kehetian

DEDICATION

In dedicating "Giants of the Earth" to the people of Armenia I also dedicate this memoir to my dear cousin, the late Rev. Fr. Vartan Kassabian. In doing so I am expressing to our family and friends that he was the inspiration which convinced me to complete my mission. At a national Armenian youth sports gathering in Detroit in September 2008, I told Der Vartan that my memoir was near completion. We embraced and his words were: "Good. Do it for our people of Armenia and our ancestors who were massacred in the now forgotten genocide."

Our Lord had other plans for my 51-year-old cousin. Der Vartan died March 12, 2009. In the 17 years he served the Armenian Church, Der Vartan was a pillar of faith for our people. Mission accomplished Der Vartan. Rest in Peace

PROLOGUE TO GIANTS OF THE EARTH

Growing up in Detroit's Armenian community was a blessing I learned to appreciate in my later years—especially after having journeyed in 1969 to the historical homeland of my parents in search of a woman named Parancim—who had survived the infamous Turkish massacres that decimated the Armenian plateau.

After my journey into the barren, depopulated homeland of my ancestors, I also learned to embrace the message of hope penned by Pulitzer Prize winning author William Saroyan. The pride of Fresno, California had decreed in a commentary focusing on Armenian pride that he did not see how any power of the world could destroy "this small tribe of unimportant people." With the stroke of his pen Saroyan etched an everlasting message for Armenians worldwide: "Go ahead, destroy Armenia. See if you can do it. Send them into the desert without bread and water. Burn their homes and churches. Then see if they will not laugh, sing and pray again. For when two of them meet anywhere in the world, see if they will not create a New Armenia."

Now I can add my testimony to Saroyan's faith in our people. In the eight days I went from village to village in Turkish-held Armenia, I can only describe my journey as having walked through a vast burial ground with no gravestones to tell the curious that the Armenian people lived on those lands for 2,000 years until the execution of the genocide of 1915.

After my mission to Turkish-held Armenia I returned to then Soviet Armenia three more times to restore my faith in life and humanity. Never did I imagine that one day little Soviet Armenia would be a free nation, and sit as a member of the United Nations. But hope has taught me miracles do happen, as evidenced in 1991 with the collapse of Soviet communism and subsequently the granting of freedom for Armenia and the Baltic States of Latvia, Estonia and Lithuania, Ukraine, Russia, Georgia, Azerbaijan, and the Soviet republics in Central Asia.

Though present-day Armenia is but a mere fragment of historical Armenia, she lives again as a free, independent nation within the majestic shadows of towering Mt. Ararat, where it is said in the Scriptures that Noah's Ark came to rest after the Great Flood. The "giants of the earth" of present-day Armenia, a nation of three million tucked in a patch of land and rugged mountains less than 12,000 square miles, can trace their roots to the Turkish-held Armenian districts of Van, Erzurum, Bitlis, Sepastia, Erzinjan, Keghi, Kharpet, Malatya, Sassoun and Moush—which had been included in the boundaries of a New Armenia drafted in 1920 for the League of Nations by Woodrow Wilson, then president of the United States. But the greedy powers of Europe turned their backs on Armenia at the Treaty of Lausanne. By their conniving misdeeds Wilson's mandate for an Armenian homeland collapsed to the glee of Mustafa Kemal Ataturk and the Turkish military.

In the chapters ahead I will share with you my meeting of fate in 1968 with the old Armenian woman in Moscow who begged I deliver a message that a woman from my father's village of Khoops—by the name of "Parancim"—had survived the Turkish massacres of 1915. That her two brothers saw Parancim before repatriating in 1947 to Soviet Armenia. I'll also share the pain that prevailed throughout my journey into historical Armenia—the same kind of pain any Armenian would have endured had they walked the same path I did in search of my Armenian roots in 1969.

On returning to my home in Detroit after walking the barren paths of the genocide of my people, I spent the next five years traveling to Armenian communities in America and Canada to show my slides of Turkish-held Armenia. I felt compelled to share them with Armenians who had escaped the carnage of 1915-23 and for their children to witness the nightmare their parents had been forced to suffer and witness in the rape of historical Armenia.

As I relived the pain and suffering of my people during every program, I was encouraged to turn my personal memoir into a book to reach out to those who believe as I do that until justice is achieved the 1.5 million massacred Armenians will be remembered in the archive of failed justice as victims of the forgotten genocide.

When Adolph Hitler ordered the execution of six million European Jews during World War II, justice eventually prevailed at the Nuremburg Trials—though it did little to lessen the Nazi Party's heinous crime against humanity. For the 1.5 million Armenians massacred by the Ottoman Turkish government there was no Nuremburg Trial. Unlike the Jewish Holocaust, the Armenian Genocide took place on the historical homeland of the Armenian people. Yet in 1969 as I went from village to village where my people lived and died, I could not even find a grave marker. To this very day in time the Turkish government denies that genocide had been orchestrated by the Ottoman government's Young Turk movement. But with each passing day we hear of courageous Turks in the country's press and universities now raising apologetic questions about "what happened in 1915?" They call it "the great catastrophe."

Even now it remains a crime in Turkey to raise the issue of the Armenian genocide in the media or in the country's schools of higher learning.

That's why I've decided to publish this memoir about my search for the woman named Parancim. Rather than rewrite my original work to conform with the present political situation in Armenia and the world, I've left those chapters of my memoir intact, and my meeting of fate in 1968 with the old Armenian woman in Moscow who inspired my search for Parancim and journey into the historical lands of my parents.

My knowledge of what transpired in Turkish-held Armenia in 1915 comes from having talked to survivors of the genocide and having read the chilling account as reported in the 684-page British Bluebook, published in 1916 under the authority of His Majesty, and entitled "The Treatment of Armenians in the Ottoman Empire, 1915-16, by Viscount Bryce." In the historical summary of that first genocide of the 20th century, the documented British Bluebook states: "There is no dispute as to what happened in 1915. The Armenian inhabitants of the Ottoman Empire were everywhere uprooted from their homes, and deported to the unhealthiest districts that the Government could select for them. It is damning evidence that the procedure itself, which set into motion all the other forces of evil, was conceived and organized by the Central Government at Constantinople. It was a deliberate, systematic attempt to eradicate the Armenian population throughout the Ottoman Empire."

As you delve into the pages ahead, you'll read how at the time I drafted my initial manuscript, Presidents Jimmy Carter, and Gerald Ford had acknowledged their statements about the crimes Turkey inflicted on the Armenians. Since then President Ronald Reagan, in addressing the murder of the Jews at the dedication of the Holocaust Museum in Washington, D.C., said "like the genocide of the Armenians before it, and the genocide of the Cambodians which followed it—and like too many other persecutions of too many other peoples—the lessons of the Holocaust must never be forgotten."

While Presidents Bill Clinton and George W. Bush expressed similar statements of remembrance to honor the massacred Armenians, they eventually bowed to the cult of genocide denial in Ankara.

Clinton recalled the events of 1915 as "one of the saddest chapters in the history of this century, the deportations and massacres of a million and a half Armenians in the Ottoman Empire in the years 1915-23;" while Bush in a campaign letter to prominent Armenian Americans wrote that the "twentieth century was marred by wars of unimaginable brutality, mass murder and genocide. History records that the Armenians were the first people of the last century to have endured these cruelties." Yet when Clinton and Bush took office as president, they shunned at using the term of genocide. How sad for the United States of America that our two world leaders would succumb to the whirling dervish Turkish lobby in Washington. Nor should we forget the action taken by the U.S. House on April 8, 1975 in which Congress voted with overwhelming support for the passage of a resolution designating April 24, 1975 as "National Day of Remembrance of Man's Inhumanity to Man," especially those of Armenian ancestry who succumbed to the genocide perpetrated in 1915." At the urging of the U.S. State Department, "in Turkey" was stricken from the congressional resolution. Again, a slap at human rights to appease the blackmailing Turkish lobbyists.

For the Turkish government denial of the 1915 genocide will not cease with time. It must recognize historic truth and condemn those in the old corrupt Ottoman Empire that carried out Turkey's crime against humanity—and rectify the sins carried out against the short-lived independent Armenian Republic of 1918, which the United States had recognized as a sovereign state.

Why is it important for Turkey to correct its past sins? Armenians in the Diaspora did not choose to scatter to all the friendly nations in the world. In my lifetime I have achieved a series of personal goals and honors in my life. I've dined at the White House, at the Governor's Mansion in Michigan, and I've been blessed with a lifetime companion who has pulled me through my share of medical scares, who gave birth to our three beautiful daughters—Grace, Janet and Karen—grandchildren, nieces and nephews and guided me to achieve a rewarding life as a professional journalist for 50 years—and yes, to have survived in a small plane crash in Ohio while on assignment for my newspaper. I can not say, nor would I, ever declare how happy I am my parents escaped the Turkish massacres so they could come to America to provide me with the good life I have been granted. For me to enjoy the freedom and good life that comes with being an American, I must never forget 1.5 million Armenians were massacred, while another 500,000 survived as refugees and orphans in the Armenian Genocide. That was the price my people paid to grant me the freedom I have been able to enjoy and cherish as an American born Armenian. Yes, I am proud to be an American by birth, but more so I am thankful to God to have been given life with the soul of an Armenian.

That's why as an Armenian American I remain dedicated to the Armenian Cause. I do it for the more than one million who were victims in the Armenian Genocide. For Armenian Americans in 2008 the election of Barack Obama as this nation's first African-American president fueled renewed hope that justice will finally come with the

Obama presidency. In campaign messages to Armenian Americans, Obama pledged to recognize the Armenian Genocide as president, while clearly spelling out his "firmly held conviction that the Armenian Genocide is not an allegation, a personal opinion, or a point of view, but rather a widely documented fact supported by an overwhelming body of historical evidence. The facts are undeniable." The former U.S. senator from Illinois was emphatic that "America deserves a leader who speaks truthfully about the Armenian Genocide and responds forcefully to all genocides, I intend to be that President."

Turkey will certainly lobby Obama to refrain from ever using the term of genocide while serving as president, claiming to do so would harm U.S.-Turkish relations, and deter any conciliatory movement between Yerevan and Ankara. Turkey successfully pulled the same blackmail diplomacy of denial with Presidents Clinton and Bush, who after winning the presidency bowed to the Turkish lobby and its pals in the U.S. State Department by refusing to term the Ottoman Turkish crime of 1915 as an act of genocide.

If the Ottoman Turkish government was able to remove the entire Armenian population through massacres and deportation in the time span of 1915-23, then please tell me, what should be the written word? It was GENOCIDE.

By adhering to his pledge that he will speak "truthfully about the Armenian Genocide" during his presidency, Barack Obama can fulfill the call for justice President Wilson had championed for the Armenian people. However, in the first 100 days of his presidency Obama retreated from the pledge by utilizing the Armenian expression "Meds Yeghern" in place of calling it "Genocide" in the President's April 24, 2009 statement on Armenian Remembrance Day. The Armenian dictionary equivalent for "Meds Yeghern" is interpreted to mean "Great Calamity."

Mr. President it was "Genocide." You said so in your run for the presidency. In the White House statement you said "my view of that history has not changed," and then you stressed that "each year we pause to remember the 1.5 million Armenians who were subsequently massacred or marched to their death in the final days of the Ottoman

Empire." Who made them march? They marched "to their death" on the orders of a government decree. That's why it was "Genocide." In your same presidential statement, you reiterate "I have consistently stated my own views of what occurred in 1915, and my view of that history has not changed."

Mr. President. It was Genocide. Fulfill your pledge to honor the 1.5 million massacred Armenians. Do not stain your presidency with Turkey's denial of guilt.

Please join me now as we share this memoir I've entitled "Giants of the Earth."

DEPARTMENT OF STATE
AIRGRAM

FILE DESIGNATION: CA-3384

HANDLING INDICATOR: LIMITED OFFICIAL USE

TO: ADANA, ANKARA

FROM: Department of State

DATE: Jul 17 10 21 AM '69

SUBJECT: Constituent Travel

REF:

Congressman Lucien N. Nedzi (Mich) has informed Dept. travel plans his good friend and constituent Mr. Mitch Kehetian Managing Editor The Community News of Detroit Michigan.

Mr. Kehetian (an American Armenian) is planning to visit various cities in Eastern Turkey once heavily populated by Armenians -- Sivas, Kigi, Erzurum, Erzincan, Mus, Bitlis, Van, Kars, Ardahan and Mt. Ararat during the period July 15-August 5. (FYI - He has discovered that a relative survived Turkish massacres several decades ago and is desirous of visiting these historic sites. He is also aware of the problems in travelling within this area. END FYI)

Embassy
He has requested/assistance in arranging travel into as many of the above areas as possible during this time period and also requests a guide for him during this journey all expenses to be paid by kxmx Mr. Kehetian.

Request Embassy guidance as to above travel request.

END

ROGERS

Drafted By: H-JBunn 6/16/69 8195
Clearances: NEA/TUR Cash
H-NEA/KNFolger

CHAPTER ONE

High on a mountaintop overlooking the western tributary of the Biblical Euphrates River in Turkish-held Armenia, I found a crude, rocky gravesite...and the soul of my Armenian heritage.

As I bowed to pray at this gravesite before me, the prayers from my lips gave way to a burning hate in my heart—a hate that appealed to God to destroy those responsible for the rape, murder and destruction of my ancestral homeland.

Even as I attempt to record that day of July 24, 1969—now in the warmth and safety of my home—my thoughts still drift back to that lonely day at a gravesite of thoughts and questions which remain unanswered.

Out there in that desolate patch of earth called Kutluja...I found Parancim. My year-long search had brought me to her crude, rocky mountaintop gravesite—and I wept for the restless souls of barren, ravaged historical Armenia.

How did I get here? What compelling force led me to this monument to historical Armenia...a monument of broken rocks stacked atop Parancim's grave? The minutes I spent at her gravesite seemed a lifetime...and in that span of despair my thoughts reflected back to the day Uncle Mesrop told me that in 1922 he learned the Turks killed Parancim. "Why do you bring me news from the grave," my aged uncle wept.

The story of my search for Parancim is a story of Armenia, and the preservation of a heritage the Ottoman Turks set out to destroy during the infamous Turkish massacres of 1915-23 that swept through the heartland of historical Armenia...and the village of Khoops in Keghi Province.

In those dark years during the height of World War I, the then government of Ottoman Turkey decided to settle the Armenian Question once and for all—under the guise of national security. When the butchering Turks wiped their blood-soaked hands, more than one million Armenians had fallen victim to massacre and starvation during the forced exodus into the deserts of Syria—and certain death for the survivors.

Parancim survived the dastardly plan of genocide engineered by the Ottoman Turks—only to die a lonely death in a land once the homeland of the Armenians. A plan of genocide which today's so-called civilized Turk still refutes, though condemned by all men and women of justice.

My journey of despair to Parancim's mountaintop gravesite was arranged by a meeting of fate with an old Armenian woman on the night of July 18, 1968 at the Metropole Hotel in Moscow—the sprawling center of Soviet communism.

Even now, I firmly believe that the hand of God arranged that meeting of fate with Arousig Mangoian. I can offer no other logical explanation. This meeting of fate I speak of was driven by two compelling desires. For my wife Rose, the stop in Moscow was the last leg of a long journey that would take her to the Armenian Soviet Republic to meet her only living aunt and scores of cousins scattered about in the small Armenian Republic.

But for me, the journey to Soviet Armenia was one driven by skepticism; and more so, to convince my prejudiced conviction that the heritage of Armenia was dying in little Soviet Armenia...a mere territorial fragment of historical Armenia. I must confess I was envious. I was envious because I had no one waiting for me in Armenia. I had been told my cousins, my aunts, my uncles—had died during the massacres of 1915.

We arrived in Moscow on the night of July 17, 1968. After the typical Soviet manner of waiting—and questioning, our group from America passed customs inspection. We boarded Intourist buses, and now it was on to Moscow and a hotel named Metropole.

By the time we arrived at our hotel, the hour was late and the director of our tour group suggested we stay in our rooms. The following morning we were treated to a typical Russian breakfast, and lectured to stay with our group at all times. The members of our group, American Armenians, were also advised to turn in our passports. The Russian Intourist guide said it was for our protection. I didn't believe her. But we had no option but to follow instructions.

Shortly after breakfast we were told to board two waiting buses in front of the hotel for a sight-seeing tour of Moscow. I wasn't interested and convinced Rose that we should go out into Moscow on our own. I wanted to see Moscow on my own and without someone telling me how great the Russians are and how great communism has been to the Soviet people and the three million Armenians who live in Soviet Armenia.

To our amazement, the warmth of the Russian people repeatedly caught me off guard—especially when I explained we were American Armenians who had come to the Soviet Union to visit Soviet Armenia. I still remember the friendly Russian traffic officer on duty in the Red Square, who offered a handshake of friendship when he learned we were headed for Yerevan, the capital city of Soviet Armenia. "The Armenian is a true brother of the Russian. He fought with us to destroy the Nazis. The poor Armenian has been fighting for centuries to retain his identity. You will be proud of your Armenian heritage when you visit Yerevan. The Armenians still live. They survived the first genocide. You will be proud of your people."

Before parting, our Russian friend advised we visit the Armenian Ararat restaurant while in Moscow. "The Ararat is filled with warmth and hospitality. The Armenian is a real host. They are a credit to the Soviet Union," he bellowed for other tourists to hear—as we stood in the shadows of the Kremlin Wall.

The setting for the meeting of fate with Arousig Mangoian was now in motion. Heeding the advice of the Russian traffic officer, we decided to spend the evening at this Armenian Ararat restaurant in Moscow.

When we met our tourist group from America, we were warned: "Everyone is asking about you. Where did you two go? You'll get in trouble." Of course, I was not about to tell them of our plans to dine at the Ararat. Later that night, while waiting for the elevator doors to open at the fourth floor level, a familiar face stared at me. It was Hamayag Kachadoorian.

My Armenian friend, now residing with his family in Los Angeles, was also bound for Armenia to visit with relatives. Hamayag had just arrived in Moscow with an Armenian tour group from California—and out of the entire group, Hamayag was the only one sent to stay at the Metropole. There was no room for Hamayag at the Ukraine Hotel.

After a lengthy chat in the hallway, I then learned that Hamayag had been assigned Room 4033. My room was 4031. I learned that the California group included 67 persons—but Hamayag had no room and was sent to the Metropole, and assigned next to my room. Again, the hand of fate was at work. My friend begged we join him for a glass of Armenian cognac, to toast our surprise meeting and the circumstances that led to our reunion at the doors of a fourth floor elevator.

I promised Hamayag we'd join him for that toast of Armenian cognac later. I explained that Rose and I were headed for the Ararat restaurant, and would visit with him on our return.

Hamayag came to America in 1947 under the sponsorship of a worldwide Armenian relief organization, founded by San Francisco restaurant owner-businessman George Mardikian. ANCHA (Armenian National Committee to Aid Homeless Armenians) was dedicated to help relocate displaced Russian Armenians who had survived the Nazi slave labor camps of World War II.

Upon Hamayag's arrival in Detroit, he was greeted by my parents, then volunteer members of the relief organization. Hamayag's first night in his new homeland was at my parents' home in Detroit's old Delray community—then a melting pot of Polish, German, Hungarian, Slovenian and Armenian Americans.

After returning from the Ararat restaurant, we went to Hamayag's room—for that promised cognac toast and the final link to a meeting of fate that would take me to Parancim's rocky gravesite overlooking the western tributary of the Euphrates River.

With Hamayag were his wife's sister, and a young Armenian woman, who had been accompanied on the visit to Moscow from the Russian city of Rostov by her aging mother Arousig Mangoian.

As Hamayag and I sipped on our cognac from Armenia, the old smiling Armenian woman asked my wife about my nationality. She had doubts if I was an Armenian—probably because I spoke in English with Hamayag and I happen to resemble the forgotten pre-Biblical Armenian, the Urartuans. I turned to this old lady and in my limited Armenian tried to assure her I was an Armenian and that my mother was born in Erzurum and my father in the village of Khoops...two old Armenian communities now a part of Turkey. When the old lady heard the name Khoops, she jumped out of her chair. Shrieking with joy, she embraced me and said "My blue-eyed Armenian son. I was born in Khoops. Tell me, what is your father's name? Are there any other sons and daughters of Khoops living in your country?"

When I explained that my father had died several years ago, that only a handful of the old timers from Khoops still live, she then asked: "Tell me. What are their names?"

To begin with, Arousig Mangoian did not know my father—but she knew my father's cousin, Uncle Mesrop. This sweet old Armenian woman then proceeded to tell me how she escaped from the Turks. How Russian soldiers saved her from the Turks...and left her with Armenians in Yerevan.

Arousig remembered Uncle Mesrop vividly. "Your uncle's father was the doctor of our village. When I was a little girl, your uncle's father mended my broken arm. When you return to America, tell Mesrop that his cousin Parancim is still alive. Tell him my two brothers who left Turkey in 1947, saw Parancim in Keghi. She survived the massacres."

The hour was now approaching midnight. We excused ourselves, for in five short hours we would be up to prepare for an early morning flight to Yerevan. I knew Arousig Mangoian would be returning to Rostov, and that I would never see this old woman again. With tears of happiness filling her weary eyes, she said to me: "Goodbye my blue-eyed son of Khoops. Do not forget me, and tell my people in your city in America Arousig still lives. I am from the Derderian family. Tell them Parancim is alive."

At that time I had no knowledge of this woman's importance to me, for the future, and for the remaining days of my life. I knew I'd see Hamayag in Yerevan, but never again would I see Arousig Mangoian. That night I slept restlessly. In the morning I told my wife about a dream. I dreamed my father was still alive, and Arousig Mangoian was in my dream. She was happy.

Two hours later we were at the airport. In less than four hours of flying time we would arrive in Yerevan—where Rose would spend 17 days with her Aunt Almast and scores of cousins from the Taline region of Soviet Armenia. I was envious.

In a short time we were air bound. The steady roar of the old prop-driven plane was unnerving, but it didn't bother Rose. She knew there would be a welcoming delegation of cousins to greet her at the airport in Yerevan, but none for me.

For Rose, the next 17 days proved to be exciting and joyful. Not only did she find cousins from her mother's side of the family, but from her father's too. They came from Irind, Taline, Kirovakan, and Batum, a Georgian Black Sea port city.

For me, there was towering Mt. Ararat, the legendary landing mountain post for the Biblical Noah's Ark. Each morning I peered out at Ararat, inspired by her beauty. And each day as my eyes turned to capture Ararat's frozen ice cap, it appeared to be beckoning as a light of everlasting eternal hope to all Armenians...now scattered to the four corners of this planet we call earth.

While Rose enjoyed each day with her cousins, I tried not to express the envy in my heart—for I knew that my cousins died in that vast stretch of land beyond towering Mt. Ararat. I knew that the families of my mother and father had perished along with the cities of Khoops and Erzurum during the genocide of 1915.

I must confess, I found little Soviet Armenia to be most exhilarating. The Armenian had survived, and as stated by the Russian traffic officer in Moscow, a sense of pride was developing within me. It was pride in seeing my people prosper and develop...basic human rights my forefathers had been denied in Turkish-held Armenia. I found myself falling in love with Yerevan, and for the first time a feeling that there is such a place called Armenia.

I think the best lesson I learned in Soviet Armenia came on the day we were to leave Yerevan. At the airport, my eyes again turned to Ararat. I wanted one more final look at that great Biblical mountain of hope the Armenians cling to, as they recall the past and near death of Armenia in 1915.

Rose's cousin, Vagharshak Nikoian, a strong and proud Armenian who tills the soil of Taline, noticed my feelings of sadness at leaving Yerevan and Mt. Ararat. Though the victim of failing eyesight, he said to me: "Feast on Ararat. One day you will feel her beauty in your heart. For out there in the hills and valleys of old Armenia, our people perished to preserve an identity. They died so that today, in new Armenia, we can work for the future of our people. Come back again to this small patch of land we call Armenia, for this is your heritage and our children's future."

As we wished each other well, and embraced for a final farewell, I sensed the message Vagharshak was trying to convey. The meaning of being an Armenian had come to fold. Now I knew why the Armenians of Soviet Armenia are so damned proud of their little country. They survived hell on earth in 1915, and now envisioned a greater future.

When we entered the plane, I searched for a seat to get one more glimpse of Ararat...and I wept. I did because I knew that out there beyond the towering ice cap of Ararat more than one million of my ancestors died in the first genocide of the 20th Century. Soon we were airborne, and I got that final glimpse. I closed my eyes and rested back in my seat. My throat and heart were burning. I felt something was missing. There was a strange feeling within me. Rose cried too, but her tears were for the cousins she left at the airport—and the 17 joyful days spent with blood relatives.

On our return to Moscow, we stayed at the Metropole hotel. We were tired and there was nothing left to see. In the morning that would follow, we would head for home...and my visit with Uncle Mesrop in Detroit.

Four days after my return to Detroit, I went to see Uncle Mesrop. I went to deliver the message from Arousig Mangoian that Parancim survived the massacres. At first I told Uncle Mesrop about our visit to Yerevan, and how inspired we were over the development of little Armenia into a healthy nation—physically and culturally. Then I told him about my strange meeting with an old Armenian woman named Arousig, and her message. That she was the Derderian girl who broke her arm. Yes, he remembered the Derderian family of Khoops.

But he stopped smiling when I gave him Arousig's message. Uncle Mesrop turned pale. He began to perspire. Then he said, in a wavering voice: "Don't believe them. She's dead. The Turks killed Parancim in 1922. Forget what the old woman told you. Why do you bring me news from the grave? Parancim is dead."

But uncle, I pleaded; this woman said her brothers saw this Parancim in 1947. Maybe she still lives. Again, Uncle Mesrop shot back: "We learned in 1922 the Turks killed Parancim. I got a letter from an Armenian living in Istanbul. He said Parancim was dead."

Now my curiosity was raised. I asked Uncle Mesrop: "If Parancim was your cousin, surely she was a cousin to my father. How close was the relation? Were they second or third cousins?"

With tears in his eyes, Uncle Mesrop said: "Didn't you know. Parancim was your father's sister."

I sat stunned. I felt sick. Parancim was my aunt. She was my father's youngest sister. I begged Uncle Mesrop to tell me more about Parancim, but he persisted that I forget the report of her being alive. When I left Uncle Mesrop's home that night, I left in a state of shock. That night turned into the longest night of my life. Rose tried to console me. Repeatedly she said, "If the old woman in Moscow was telling the truth, and if she was certain that the Parancim her brothers saw was your father's sister—what can we do?"

That night, a million thoughts flashed through my mind. If Parancim still lives how in the world will I find her? All we know is she was last seen in 1947 in Keghi, the county seat of my father's village of Khoops— an old Armenian city nestled up against the Sulbuz mountain range overlooking the Euphrates River in the remote interior of Turkish-held Armenia.

Despite Uncle Mesrop's insistence Parancim died a horrible death in 1922; I convinced myself, out of sheer faith and desperation—that Aunt Parancim still lives, 21 years after being seen alive. I wrote about my hopeful discovery in a group of community newspapers I then managed on Detroit's east side.

My story brought offers of help to complete the search for Parancim. The voices of help and hope came from readers and friends. It was a search that ended July 24, 1969 on a mountaintop gravesite overlooking the Euphrates River.

I found Parancim's grave.

CHAPTER TWO

An old Armenian woman I met in Moscow tells me Parancim was seen alive in 1947. Uncle Mesrop insists the Turks killed Parancim in 1922.

I wanted to believe the old Armenian woman. I did. I wrote it that way for my newspaper. The headline expressed my faith: "Like a voice from the grave: Learns his Aunt is alive." Then the phone calls came from readers. With each call, my faith grew stronger Parancim still lives.

A few days after the story appeared in the newspaper, an offer of help came from Detroit Congressman Lucien N. Nedzi. The congressman said: "I read your story. It sounds like a miracle. Please let me help you find your Aunt Parancim. If she still lives, we'll find her."

But where do I start. I knew so little about my father's family history—let alone the conditions that prevailed in the village of Khoops; when the Turkish minister of interior, Talaat, sent out the orders in April of 1915 to execute the Ottoman Turkish plan of genocide against the Armenians.

Congressman Nedzi suggested I talk to every known survivor of my Aunt Parancim's village—to attain as much personal information as humanly possible. There was one person I knew who could help, Mrs. Arousig Topelian. According to several old timers of Khoops, Mrs. Topelian was the last person to see Aunt Parancim. When I called my father's cousin that Aunt Parancim might still be alive, she wept.

She wept because she was the last person to see Aunt Parancim. When I told Mrs. Topelian of the message I brought back from Moscow, a message Uncle Mesrop refused to heed, she said: "After all these years. I can't believe it. May the Almighty God listen to your prayers."

At my urging, Mrs. Topelian relived those dark days of April 1915—when genocide swept through Khoops village like a plague of locusts devouring the countryside. As she related each incident leading to the massacres, it seemed as if the holocaust of 1915 had entered Mrs. Topelian's body. Trembling, and in tears, she told me the story—a story of despair and agony for the survivors. Arousig Keteian Topelian's story follows:

"It was mid April in 1915 when notices were posted in Khoops that all men, women and children were to prepare for a long journey. The notice made it clear that only the old men would join the women and children. All young men were to report for military service—to serve the Turkish army in the war against the enemy; namely, Great Britain, France, Italy, and Russia. Several days after the young men were taken from our village, we heard of their deaths. On the road leading to Bingol, the Turks opened fire on the defenseless Armenians...the bloodbath had begun.

"Next they came for the old men, the women, and the children. As we were driven along the Euphrates River toward Kutluja, the Turkish soldiers said we would rest. But it was not to be so. The sun was setting when I heard the cries of mercy. I saw blood everywhere. I saw them kill my family. I saw them kill babies. I saw them rape girls, as the blood dripped from their knives.

"The friendly Kurds of Kutluja tried to intercede, but were driven back by the Turks. Within minutes the once golden winter wheat fields of Kutluja had turned red from the blood of my people. .

"I started to run for the thick fields in the hillside. Parancim was a few steps behind me. She fell. I kept running. When I turned to look for Parancim, the Turkish soldiers had grabbed her by the hair. I wanted to go back to help Parancim, but I was afraid. There was death everywhere. I ran until I fell to the ground. With all my strength I crawled for cover under some heavy brush...and hid there all night. When daylight came, I heard some voices. They were the voices of Armenians. These Armenians were being taken to Kharpet. I joined them. Several days later we had reached Kharpet. The city was crowded with old men, women and children. Their destination was the Syrian desert of Der el Zor, the hot sands of certain death. The

American Christian Mission in Kharpet persuaded the Turkish soldiers to leave the children at the mission. I had been saved. Thank God for the Americans.

"But I had lost my family. And to this very day I still see Parancim on the ground surrounded by Turkish soldiers. The scars of that day will go with me to the grave. Now you tell me Parancim may still be alive. Dear God, let it be true she still lives."

By now Mrs. Topelian had relived hell on earth. I felt sick myself. I felt remorse at having forced this old woman who I respect as an aunt, to relive a horrifying experience from her youth. She then told me about my father's family, and described how Parancim looked—that dark day in 1915 before the Turks came.

Mrs. Topelian's passport to safety came with the blessing of the American Near East Relief Committee. After Turkey's surrender to the then Allied Powers, the Committee published a list of all surviving Armenian children at the Kharpet mission—in a Boston, Massachusetts Armenian language newspaper. Elder friends of my father saw Arousig Keteian's name on the list. Quickly they sent for the "sole surviving Armenian of Khoops Village."

Each day hundreds of Armenian orphans were being rescued from the interior of Turkey. Ottoman Turkey was in disarray. Her Turkonic dream of a vast empire connecting the Baghdad rail link with Berlin had collapsed. Her main ally, Germany had surrendered. The Turks blamed their defeat on the Armenians.

The first report on Aunt Parancim's whereabouts came in 1921. A Turkish merchant in Istanbul told Armenians there that an Armenian girl by the name Parancim Keteian, from Khoops village, was being held captive in village of Kutluja. But the surviving Keteian family members in Detroit were skeptical of the report. Many Armenians who had escaped the massacres to reach the shores of New York were being tricked by fortune-seeking Turkish merchants of greed, who, for a price, claimed they could get Armenians out of the interior. But they never fulfilled their contracts of greed and despair. By now travel in the interior had become impossible. Mustafa Kemal Ataturk had taken power—and turned his hate against the remaining Greeks and Armenians still scattered in the vast, barren depopulated interior.

A year after the first report on Aunt Parancim, Uncle Mesrop heard from an Armenian in Istanbul. The Armenian letter writer claimed Aunt Parancim was dead—that she had been slain by her Turkish abductors while attempting to flee Kutluja. But my father, Kaspar, and his brother, Dikran, always spoke of their blue-eyed sister. I never questioned them. I assumed they were speaking of a sister who died during the massacres. Even the name, Parancim, meant little to me...until Uncle Mesrop told me about Parancim.

After my visit with Mrs. Topelian, I talked to other senior members of the Khoops community in Detroit—seeking to uncover the kind of information I need to help me in my search. I cringed when others told me they made no attempt to attain positive verification that Parancim was dead. They merely accepted the word of an Armenian merchant in Istanbul; who in 1922, sent a letter to Uncle Mesrop. I damned myself for failing to ask these kinds of questions on my family tree while my parents were alive. In my job as a reporter I always asked questions, but like so many children we think our parents will live forever. Whenever I discussed the massacres with my father, he cried. He did because his story was one of despair—the same story thousands of other Armenian fathers told their children when questioned about the fate of their forefathers.

I knew my father and Uncle Dikran came to America in 1912. Uncle Dikran was the older of the two brothers. The plan was to raise enough money to send for the remaining members of the Keteian family...still in Khoops. In early 1915, my father's father, Nishan, came to America. He brought another son, Philibos, who was ailing with a visual disease. Philibos was losing his sight. My grandfather thought doctors in Boston could save his son's eyesight. He was told there was no chance to save his son from blindness.

The news from Armenia was bleak. Disturbances were taking place in the interior. News reports were focusing on a Turkish plan to remove the Armenians from the interior—and Khoops was right in the interior zone. My grandfather Nishan announced that he and Philibos were going back to Armenia—to keep the family together. But my grandfather insisted that his sons Kaspar and Dikran stay in America, until safer conditions returned to Armenia. When they boarded a ship bound for the old world, they were never to be heard from again.

I think this is what really got to my father's emotions when I would raise the question of the massacres. He would say: "They went back to die."

My first break on getting personal information on Aunt Parancim came from Hovannes Vosgerichian, one of the driving forces of the Patriotic Union of Khoops—an organization of American Armenians who came from the village of Khoops. When I told Mr. Vosgerichian about the message from Moscow—from Arousig Mangoian—he smiled. "Of course I knew her. I knew the Derderian family. You say she is alive. We thought she died in the massacres. If she says Parancim is alive, you must pursue the question. My God, if she still lives…we must bring her to America."

He then told me Aunt Parancim had been promised in marriage to a Dikran Kostegian, an Armenian from the village of Khoops. Kostegian came to America in 1914—also in search of work to send for his sweetheart, Aunt Parancim.

When World War I broke out on the European continent, Turkey was allied with Germany—but throughout the war, Turkey and the United States never engaged in conflict. Many of the Armenians who arrived in America, joined the U.S. Army—thinking they would battle the Turks., but that chance never came…even for my father who joined the army while working on the railroad in Montana. But Dikran Kostegian went to Canada instead. He joined the British military…because Great Britain was at war with Turkey.

My father's service stint got him as far as Fort Wayne, then a military base on the foot of the Detroit River near the Delray neighborhood I was born and raised. Dikran Kostegian's fortunes took him to Palestine to join forces with the British Gen. Edmund Allenby. Somewhere on the plains of old Palestine, Dikran Kostegian gave his life for a cause he revered—to free Armenia from Turkish rule and oppression, and to embrace his childhood sweetheart, Parancim.

Dikran Kostegian's heroics are etched in a book on the history of Khoops. He died on Palestinian soil. He died fighting the Turks.

After gathering what I could on the life of Parancim, I returned to visit with Mrs. Topelian—and on her encouragement, I began to give serious consideration at going to Turkey—to the ancestral homeland of the Armenian people. "If you go, please be careful. The Turks hate our people. But you must go, you must find out once and for all if Parancim lives. You must find out for yourself. What your Uncle Mesrop was told in 1922 may have been a false report." Mrs. Topelian added.

After linking together all the bits and pieces of information, some of it hearsay—I wrote to Congressman Nedzi. It was a history of my Aunt Parancim, with information to help the American Embassy in Ankara to conduct the search. I was thrilled when the congressman said he would request embassy assistance in the search. "This is the only way. It would be impossible for you. Even if you went, where would you go? What would you look for, and remember, you are an Armenian," Nedzi stressed.

As each week passed, a letter would always come from the congressman's office in Washington, D.C. Most often, the message read: "Proceeding on search for whereabouts of Parancim Keteian."

At one juncture, the congressman called me, inquiring why the difference in the family name spelling. There was a simple explanation. When my father completed his military service, an officer in charge of the separation detachment slipped in an "h" in the family name—on my father's discharge papers.

Then copies of communiqués came from the American consulate in Adana, in southern Turkey. With each message it seemed we were getting closer. They had been able to trace Parancim Keteian to Bingol province. Then we were told the search would be delayed through December because of heavy snowfalls in the mountains of Keghi—an old Armenian province, which includes Kutluja.

Christmas, 1968 had now passed—still no positive news. The months seemed years, as I waited for some kind of encouraging news. Several times I called the congressman, only to be told: "Be patient. Getting news about Armenians out of Turkey is a great task, but we'll do it. I promise."

Then on the morning of January 3, 1969, the long-awaited call came. I had just written a story for that week's edition of the paper on a subject of faith in the New Year—to take stock of our American ideals and to work to make this a greater land for all people.

The switchboard operator handed me a note. The note merely said "you have a long distance call on the line. I think it's from Washington. Shall I take a message or can you take your call." I grabbed the phone and shouted "for God's sake…put the call through." Congressman Nedzi was calling. His voice was faint. It wasn't the usual cheerful Nedzi. I still remember each word that followed:

"Mitch. I have some bad news. The Secretary of State has been advised by our consulate in Adana that a woman by the name Parancim Keterine, who answers the description of your aunt—died seven years ago—in the village of Kutluja."

I thought the newsroom was spinning. I asked Nedzi to repeat what he had just said. Again—"died seven years ago"—came from his lips. I began to tremble. My eyes filled. I was seven years too late.

A few minutes passed before I could talk with any sense of communicating. The congressman just waited. Then he said: "Look Mitch. I will forward you a copy of the cable report from Adana. I would imagine the cable leaves many unanswered questions. Though her last name is spelled Keterine, all indications point to the fact she is your Aunt Parancim. Upon review of this message you may wish to frame additional questions to the embassy and to the Turkish governor of Bingol province.

Though the phone went dead, I held on. Beads of perspiration formed on my forehead. I felt as if I was on fire. It seemed as if the little newsroom was moving in on me. When I looked up, my publisher, Ben Nathanson, said softly: "Mitch. Why don't you take the rest of the day off?"

Ben could understand why I grieved. He knew the tragic history of the Armenian people—he knew the Armenians were victims of the first genocide of the 20th Century. His people, the Jews, less than 25 years after the 1915 genocide destroyed Armenia, felt the terror of the Jewish

Holocaust. Six million of his people were terminated by Nazi Germany through concentration death camps in Europe.

Nathanson, recognized as a leader in Michigan's newspaper industry for having built a chain of weekly newspapers in Detroit and Macomb County, then asked: "Did Nedzi tell you about her family? Did she have any children?"

I couldn't remember. All I heard was Aunt Parancim died seven years ago. I picked up the phone, and dialed the congressman's Washington office number—but couldn't get through. Finally, the operator cut in and got the call through. The congressman was still in his office. I asked him if there was anything about a family on the cable report from Adana. The congressman said there was mention made of two children. Again I hesitated, and Nedzi said: "I know how you feel. We'll talk this over when I get back to the district next week."

Then I said something I regretted later. I wished the hell this search never started. Again my friend the congressman injected: "Whatever the reason. Something, someone got this started. It may be greater than you imagine. Sometimes fate has a strange way of plowing its course."

Heeding my publisher's advice, I left the office. There was a note of silence in the newsroom. My fellow co-workers knew of the bad news. By the time I reached my car, I began to sob as I wept at the funerals of my mother and father. It wasn't supposed to end this way. I cursed repeatedly. I drove for several hours. I didn't want to go home. I just wanted to be alone. Finally, I headed for home.

I couldn't sleep that night. It was a repeat of that night Uncle Mesrop told me Parancim was my father's sister—my aunt. I kept thinking of Uncle Mesrop insisting I forget what the old Armenian woman told me at the Metropole Hotel in Moscow: "The Turks killed Parancim. Don't believe them...she's dead."

Several days later, the cable report from Adana arrived from the congressman's office. It stated:

"Subject: Welfare Whereabouts: Keteian Parancim. Telegram report from Governor Bingol Province, Eastern Turkey. Identifies Keterine Parancim Perse from Kutluja Village, Keghi District, Bingol Province who died seven years ago. Deceased

woman survived by two children, Huseyin and Elif. If further information requested, please advise—Quinlan."

Still I refused to accept this cable report. Uncle Mesrop was wrong in 1922 and for the years that followed. The same could be true now. I wrote a short story on the State Department cable report for my newspaper, and followers of my search again called. They urged I continue. "You can't stop now. Go and see for yourself. Get solid proof. Our prayers go with you," my friends repeated after reading the story.

Again I called Congressman Nedzi. This time for his assistance in getting me permission to travel into the interior of Turkey, and some kind of protection from our Embassy in Ankara. As I expected, the congressman responded: "You just get ready. We'll have the State Department alert the American Embassy in Ankara of your plans. Don't worry, we'll get you through. We've come this far. This is no time to stop. But please be cautious when you get to Turkey. The Turks still blame the Armenians for their misfortunes during World War I.

My brothers, Phil and Nash, and sister, Isabel Kehetian-Mercurio, all urged I be cautious if I can get permission to get to historical Armenian regions in Turkey. "Don't try to be a hero. Be careful, come back safe and write about what you find," pleaded my sister, now living in Chicago.

As the weeks rolled along, additional communiqués came from Turkey. Each report confirmed the cable report from our Embassy in Ankara. Finally, on April 24, 1969 while recalling that it was on an April 24 in 1915 when the butchering Turks launched their plan of genocide...I decided I must go to Kutluja to end this mystery that started with a letter from Istanbul in 1922 reporting the death of Parancim Keteian.

When the plans were completed, the date for my departure was set for July 5, 1969. Little did I know it would be more than a search for the truth on the mystery of Aunt Parancim—it was to become a journey about finding my Armenian roots in the land of the "Giants of the Earth."

CHAPTER THREE

Though my flight plans called for a short stop in London, my stay in this majestic metropolis turned out to be an overnight stay—and much to my enjoyment. We missed the flight to Istanbul by less than 15 minutes. The apologizing airline attendant said the next flight to the Turkish capital would be the following morning. She suggested I get a quick glimpse of London that night.

Once in the airport terminal, I went to the telephone books. Surely, a city of London's magnitude would have an Armenian community. I was right. Turning to the church listings my eyes spotted "St. Sarkis Armenian Church." Quickly I dialed the church number. On the other end of the line, a young Armenian who had studied at the seminary of the Etchmiadzin Holy See in Soviet Armenia answered my call. True to Armenian tradition, the young Etchmiadzin seminarian said: "Just stay at your hotel. I'll be there in 30 minutes. You must see our church and if time allows after the choir rehearsal I will take you on a tour of beautiful London."

By the time I unpacked my overnight case, there was a knock at the door. It was the Etchmiadzin seminary student. In the drive to his church, I explained my mission to Turkey and how my journey had developed. After meeting with several members of the St. Sarkis church, my friend suggested we dine at a Greek restaurant in downtown London and then take in a few historic English sites.

As the evening wore on, I found Vrej Nersessian possessed the same nationalist Armenian spirit that burned in my heart. When the night came to the closing of our mini tour of the city, he asked: "When you reach the interior of Turkey you will come across an ancient Armenian city named Bitlis. Author William Saroyan's parents were also from Bitlis. If time permits, please visit this city—do it for me in memory of my slain ancestors."

The young aspiring church leader's family roots were linked to ancient Bitlis. I promised Vrej I would, and if possible take pictures of the city that once was home for his family. Before departing, he repeated: "May God watch over you as you walk the paths of our ancestral homeland." As the tears flowed from his reddened eyes, he blessed me with a prayer. It was a prayer of protection that he felt I would need once in the interior of historical Turkish-held Armenia.

When I returned to my room I wept because of the night spent with the young English-speaking Armenian. I wept because the story of Armenia is a story of heartbreak and tragedy—whenever two Armenians meet and compare family background. When I went to bed that night, I knew well that by the same hour the next day I would be in Turkey—and for the first time to find myself surrounded by Turks. The only Turk I had ever met was a police captain from Ankara, while carrying out my assignment as a Detroit Times reporter. The Turkish officer was visiting the Detroit police department. I had been assigned by my city editor, Jim Trainor, to interview the visitor from Turkey. I did my professional job. I never raised the Armenian question.

I must admit that the thought of being with Turks worried me some. Not out of fear, but out of fear that I might lose my control and create an incident.

In the morning I hurried about. I was not about to miss my flight to Istanbul. I wanted to get to Turkey. I wanted to find Aunt Parancim. Once at the airport terminal, I knew it was just a matter of hours when I would set foot on Turkish soil. Sure enough, hours later our plane landed at Istanbul airport. As we deplaned, I saw them. They were everywhere. The race I had learned to hate.

At that precise moment an eerie pulsation pained my heart as I recorded the imprint of the flag hanging limp from the staff atop the airport dome. It was the Turkish crescent. I was in Turkey. Once inside the airport, I was told my connecting flight to Ankara would leave in two or three hours. I just sat with thoughts racing through my mind. I was afraid. I was afraid because I knew my journey was yet to begin and I had a feeling of concern whether I could endure being with millions of Turks and not confront them about the genocide of my people. Then it came. The flight to Ankara was ready for boarding. I spoke to no one. I just rested back in my seat and reminded myself to shake loose of my inner feeling about Turks or my journey would fail. In a short time the flight attendant announced we would be landing in Ankara. Once on the ground below I picked up my two suitcases and paged a taxi. He was a friendly Turk and wished me well on my visit to Ankara.

Now I knew the time had come for the journey east—into the interior of Turkey and the ancestral homeland of the Armenian people. Then I broke out in a chill despite the intense July heat. It was a chill heightened out of fear, as my massacred ancestors endured during the Turkish plan of genocide.

For me it was a fear of what I would find out there in the eastern provinces of Turkey—in my search for Aunt Parancim.

Upon reaching the Grand Hotel in downtown Ankara, I was greeted by an English-speaking Turkish innkeeper. After inspecting my passport, he asked: "You are an American. May you enjoy your visit to our beautiful Turkey."

How I wanted to shout back that the lands he speaks of in the interior belonged to my people when his Turkish ancestors were still living in tents in central Asia. Instead, I responded that I was an American-Armenian. I came to Turkey to visit historic Armenian cities in eastern Turkey. Now the smiling innkeeper frowned. He slammed my room keys on the desk, and retorted with a caustic "good night…" I wanted to throw the fucking keys back in his face. But I was not going to let this bastard get me riled up on my first day in Turkey.

When I got to my room, I realized my curt remarks had no basis. Future outbursts might jeopardize my mission and search for Aunt Parancim. One can never imagine the thoughts that streaked through my mind as I tried to sleep that first night in Turkey. Before I turned in, I lodged a chair up against the door. It made me feel secure. Soon I fell asleep. Hours later I woke up to a clanking alarm clock. I felt at ease. I had survived my first night in Turkey. At breakfast my hostess suggested I have some toast, a cup of fruit and American coffee. She was pleasant. Everyone about seemed pleasant. Yet I kept telling myself that the ancestors of these pleasant Turks massacred my ancestors. After breakfast, I returned to my room to gather my materials on Aunt Parancim to take to the American Embassy in Ankara. Most of the correspondence in my possession had originated out of the office of U.S. Secretary of State William P. Rogers.

When I reached the American Embassy, an assistant to Ambassador William J. Handley greeted me with a friendly American welcome. When we stepped into his partially private office to discuss my journey into the interior, he advised I speak softly. "Some of our employees are Turks. They might resent an American-Armenian journalist going into the interior, a zone they desire not to discuss. Some Turks would like to forget the Armenians existed. It's like a cancer with these people. You know what I mean, don't you..."

The cordial assistant also assured me that the Embassy would use all of its available resources to secure "some reliable people to join me in the journey," and he warned: "It's too dangerous to travel alone. You can't speak Turkish and remember you are an American-Armenian. Be careful what you discuss with your Turkish guide."

While the ambassador's assistant pierced through the maze of Department of State correspondence in my possession, one document commanded his attention. It was a Department of State airgram from the office of Secretary Rogers, dated June 16, 1969, and dispatched to our American consulate in Adana and the Embassy in Ankara.

In a hushed tone, yet with firmness, he said: "This document is for official department use. How in the world did you get a copy of the airgram. Leave it with me for safe keeping. If the Turks see it, they'll cause trouble. Trouble is something we don't want . I am sure you understand the delicate situation."

Quickly I read the airgram, and for the first time recognized its delicate content. Repeatedly I assured the ambassador's assistant I would keep the document on my person at all times. Then, and only then, the embassy aide relented in his demand, and pleaded: "Please, for your own protection, do not show the airgram to anyone."

When U.S. Rep. Nedzi enlisted the aid of Secretary Rogers in the search for Aunt Parancim, the Detroit congressman kept me informed of all progress reports—including copies of information directed to his office from the Department of State. Six days prior to my departure for Turkey, I received the airgram copy which upset the embassy aide to no end.

Initially, the airgram was noted as a piece of "unclassified" correspondence. But someone had it re-classified, and in bold letters it stated: "LIMITED OFFICIAL USE." In addition, the airgram clearly defined "For Department Use Only."

Why was there an attachment of importance to that airgram in my possession? Simply, it stated the truth. Sub-head "From Department of State; Subject: Constituent Travel" the document read:

"Congressman Lucien N. Nedzi (Mich.) has informed Dept. travel plans his good friend and constituent Mr. Mitch Kehetian, Managing Editor, The Community News of Detroit, Michigan.

"Mr. Kehetian (an American Armenian) is planning to visit various cities in Eastern Turkey once heavily populated by Armenians—Sivas, Kigi, Erzurum, Erzican, Mus, Bitlis, Van, Kars, Ardahan and Mt. Ararat during the period July 15-August 5. (FYI—He has discovered that a relative survived Turkish massacres several decades ago and is desirous of visiting these historic sites. He is also aware of the problems in travelling within this area. END FYI)

He has requested Embassy assistance in arranging travel into as many of the above areas as possible during this time period and also requests a guide for him during this journey. All expenses to be paid by Mr. Kehetian.

"Request Embassy guidance as to the above travel request."

And it was signed: END ROGERS

In addition to the sign-off by Secretary Rogers, the airgram was initialed by the following department personnel: the airgram was drafted by Jacqueline Bunn, given clearance by Charlotte M. Hubbard and Kathryn N. Folger, signed by Frank E. Cash Jr., country director,

Turkey; and again signed by Jacqueline Bunn for "contents and classification."

To fully grasp the meaning and importance of Secretary Rogers' Department of State airgram, one must have a working knowledge of the meaning "TURKISH MASSACRES" as referred to by the then United States cabinet officer. In later chapters I will attempt to relive those dark days of Armenia's past as we journey through some of the "once heavily populated" Armenian cities mentioned in Secretary Rogers' airgram.

But let me touch on the airgram's significance to persons of Armenian heritage, and justice-seeking citizens of the world who still champion for an answer to the Armenian Question.

Not since the World War I administration of President Woodrow Wilson has mention been made of a "Turkish massacre" by a ranking Presidential cabinet member. Though Secretary Rogers' reference to "Turkish massacres" was not intended for public knowledge, as his airgram stated (FYI—for your information), the fact remains—it was so declared.

Members of the Congress, governors and local city officials frequently speak out against the genocide of 1915—and in doing so point the finger of guilt at the then rulers of Ottoman Turkey for having engineered the plan of extermination.

Why make such a fuss over a reference to "Turkish massacres" you ask, and rightfully so. No American president or ranking cabinet member since the Wilson days has pointed the finger of guilt at Turkey—until Rogers' remarks in the airgram.

Remarks such as the ones stressed in the secretary's airgram will upset the Turk to no end, and I intend to share it at the time I choose. It serves notice to the so-called modern Turk that the crimes of 1915 will haunt Turkey forever.

As an example, back in 1965 as American Armenians were observing the 50th year of mourning of that genocide, members of Congress from all parts of this land delivered remarks into the Congressional Record—remarks which rekindled the call for justice. One such statement was inserted by then Michigan Congressman

Gerald R. Ford. In a short and concise statement, the then congressman condemned Turkey of the 1915 "genocide of the Armenian people."

When Ford assumed the office of President, following the resignation of President Richard Nixon, I wrote to my former Michigan congressman asking if he still adhered to the epic condemnation of Turkey. In response, The White House said "the historical record of the statement seems clear"—and again the past continues to haunt Turkey.

To be precise, the President's four paragraph statement, matches the statements of the Wilson era in American politics. Though Mr. Ford made the statement as a congressman, he stuck to his condemnation as President.

At the time I pressed the President to reaffirm his statement of 1965, he was embroiled in a controversy with Congress on continuing military aide to Turkey. But even then, historical fact stood above the political scene—and President Ford responded that the "historical record of the statement seems clear."

The President's posture on the question reappeared in Armenian language newspapers in all corners of the globe—aided by Associated Press coverage. I should like to repeat Mr. Ford's statement of 1965. It reads:

"Mr. Speaker, with mixed emotion we mark the 50th anniversary of the Turkish genocide of the Armenian people.

"In taking special notice of the shocking events in 1915, we observe this anniversary with sorrow in recalling the massacres of Armenians and with pride in saluting those brave patriots who survived the attacks to fight on the side of freedom during World War I.

"The stouthearted Armenian people who escaped the terror, murder, and carnage set an example for the free world by their devotion to the cause of freedom and by their tremendous personal sacrifices.

"I join my colleagues in pausing to extend our deep sympathy to thousands of Americans whose Armenian forefathers fought for freedom with our war allies and who have given so much of themselves to make this a better country, and a strong one."

One will never imagine the pride that swept through the Armenian community in this nation and lands removed from the American scene. It proved to the world—and the Turk—that even the President of the United States of America recognizes historical fact.

President Ford was an honest sincere man. In a meeting with Panax Newspaper editors at the White House, Ford greeted me with a hearty handshake, and expressed that friendship with "and how is my Armenian friend from Michigan. Welcome to the White House."

In November, 1975 while representing my newspaper at a press conference in Detroit—with Secretary of State Henry Kissinger as the guest star—I took the opportunity to question Mr. Kissinger on the fate of a U.S. House resolution honoring the massacred Armenians, specifically if it was true that his office was trying to derail the resolution. While denying the claim, Kissinger then branded the 1915 massacres as being "tragic what happened to the Armenians 60 years ago..."

Again, recognition of historical fact.

First I referred to Secretary of State Rogers' airgram, in which clear reference was made to "cities in Eastern Turkey once heavily populated by Armenians" and his caution of "for your information" on the question of "Turkish massacres of several decades ago."

Then came President Ford's reaffirmation of a statement he made as a congressman, in which he had condemned Turkey of the genocide of the Armenian people. As president, he termed his congressional statement as "historical record."

Finally we have Secretary Kissinger's own admission that a great tragedy had taken place "60 years ago."

One could go on and on with statements of record—but the Turk refuses to acknowledge the historical fact that back in 1915 the Turkish government embarked on a plan that was to be named the first genocide of the 20th Century.

Thus you grasp the importance persons of Armenian heritage attach to statements of historical fact—especially when the statements serve as a reminder that Turkey's genocide of the Armenians be remembered by humankind.

Let us now proceed with my mission in Turkey. Before the end of the day had come, Ambassador Handley's assistant had secured for me the services of a "reliable" representative of the Turkish Ministry of Tourism. Our embassy aide was confident of my success to negotiate the journey, and gave one final warning: "Protect the papers you have from the Department of State, and check in with our office when you return. We just want to make sure all went well with you. Don't forget to check in…"

The following morning I went to the tourism office. They were expecting me. The tourism representative was friendly and seemed displeased with life in Turkey. "It's rough making a living here. I spent several years in West Germany. There I enjoyed life. What in the world compels you to visit the interior of Turkey? No tourist takes the route you want," he stated repeatedly.

After pleading the importance of my journey, and willingness to "pay any price," he said: "I shouldn't do this, but if we change some of your money on the market I think I can swing it for you." Days later I was to discover the extra profit to be realized was to line his pocket. I didn't blame him. It was a risk he was willing to take to provide me with the necessary papers to head into the interior and off the normal "tourist attraction sites."

Once the deal had been made, and the money exchanged, the Turkish tourist representative invited me to lunch. He warned: "Now you realize this trip of yours should go through a commercial agency. You might be stopped in the interior, and if it happens there is nothing I can do to help." We shook hands and agreed to meet later in the afternoon to meet my prospective guide and driver.

That afternoon I met my prospective guide. He was a political science student at the University of Ankara—and knew "some Armenians in Lebanon." The young man showed deep interest in the planned journey, and said: "Once we get into the interior, where the Armenians lived, we must ask the old Turks what really happened in 1915. Every time I visit Beirut, my Armenian friends blame my people for the tragedy that took place in the eastern provinces. Whatever happened out there between our two peoples, Turkey now suffers from the tragedy. Everyone hates us. Our country is backward and our people need work."

Then the young Turk, claiming he knew some Armenian history, said: "You have the appearance of the ancient Urartu Armenian. The Urartu Armenians were light-skinned. Many had blue eyes. You are the second such Armenian I know who resembles the Urartu. The Armenians I know in Lebanon are modern Armenians. They are dark and have dark eyes."

On his urging, I agreed to have dinner with his "Urartu Armenian friend." Meanwhile, I reminded myself to proceed with caution. The discussion was too friendly. He was too cooperative. Was this what our embassy aide was cautioning me about? The Armenian he wanted me to meet operated a small jewelry store of sorts in a central store in the poor section of Ankara. His name was Zadik.

Zadik was a small-framed man. When we were introduced, this small man's eyes came alive. We spoke in Armenian. He told me he was born in Kayseri, an old Greek city in Western Turkey. "I used to speak good Armenian, but I speak very little now. There aren't too many Armenians in Ankara. There aren't too many left in Turkey," Zadik reiterated.

Zadik praised my Turkish guide as a good man. "Your guide is an educated Turk. He has traveled. He knows the truth. You will be safe with him. May God be with you in your journey into the interior."

When we parted, Zadik called out: "My prayers go with you."

My young guide walked me to the Grand Hotel, and along the way said: "This will be a thrill for me. Not too many young Turks get to see the deep interior unless they're on military duty. We can learn from each other. We might learn not to hate as our forefathers did out there in the eastern provinces." At the hotel, we shook hands and set a meeting time for the next day at the tourism office to map our planned journey.

That night I was excited. One more day of planning and I'd be on my way. It just seemed impossible. It was like a dream. A dream American Armenians ponder about when discussing the ancestral homeland…and for me the dream was about to take the form of reality.

In the morning I hurried over to the tourism office…only to learn there had been a change in plans. The tourism representative said: "We had to get you a new guide. The other young man can't make the trip. He had forgotten about his college examinations. We have another young man who will serve as your guide." At that moment I was scared. I did not buy the story that the young man had forgotten about his examinations. I am certain the authorities had changed the guide arrangement. I thought the journey was now in jeopardy. If the young man was a government plant, I said nothing to offend him. I will never know what happened.

But I do remember the young man's comments of the previous day. He said repeatedly "On Monday I start a three week vacation. No school. No books to study. We will have a good time visiting historic Armenian cities in Anatolia," the term Turks give to the Eastern provinces.

However, I was at their mercy. I waited for my new guide to appear. Two hours after the abrupt change in plans, a young graduate of the Ankara School of Law, Nur Tanisik, walked into the office of the tourism representative. With him was Mehmet Unlu, a husky warm-hearted Kurd who was to serve as my official chauffeur and bodyguard into the interior. I did not question the change. Nothing would stop me now. I had come too far...since that meeting of fate with an old Armenian woman in Moscow.

Nur and Mehmet were most friendly, and the mood expressed by the two was a relief. But I'll always wonder why the change. Did the other young man appear too interested in the Armenians? Or was he a decoy to see if I would openly attack the Turks? My new guide outlined our course, and suggested I get plenty of rest...and admitted: "This will be an experience for me too. I've never seen the interior. We'll see you early in the morning."

And early he and Mehmet were. The two arrived at the Grand Hotel at 7 in the morning. It was Sunday, July 20, 1969. The journey was to begin. Mehmet's car was a 1955 Chevrolet. "Don't worry. My car will take you through the mountains of the Armenian plateau—where your parents once lived," Mehmet vowed.

My journey into the land of the "Giants of the Earth" had begun.

CHAPTER FOUR

In the days ahead I will relive the carnage that swept across historical Armenia. Even now I see it everywhere. No Armenians. No gravestones to tell me who lived and died on these lands. While my mission is to confirm that my Aunt Parancim had survived the massacres, this mission includes visits to the villages and towns my parents and my wife's parents were born and raised. My dream was now taking place. But it would turn out to be a nightmare…

Since our Embassy in Ankara warned me to not let the Turks know I had a copy of Secretary Rogers' airgram addressing the "Turkish massacres" I kept reading the June 16 dated airgram sensing it was a document that I needed to conceal from the Turks. The airgram was market "LIMITED OFFICIAL USE." While candidates for Congress and the White House condemn the massacres and genocide of the Armenians, to have "Turkish massacres" stated in the airgram was speaking for the United States Government—something the U.S. Department of State opposes so as not to offend the Turks, a so-called NATO ally.

Can you imagine the State Department attempting to derail a Jewish Holocaust resolution so as not to offend present-day Germany? Hell no. That kind of an act would be condemned by the U.S. Congress. It would never happen. It would be unthinkable. But now was not the time to fuel my anger. At the right time I would share the State Department airgram addressing the "Turkish massacres."

The night before I left on my mission, I re-read portions of the British Bluebook that focused on the towns Nur and Mehmet had drafted for our journey and remembered the tragic expressions like the segment about the fate of the Armenians of Sepastia, which the Turks call Sivas. The chilling account written by Viscount Bryce is still with me: "In the town of Sepastia, which comprised some 25,000 Armenians have either been killed or deported to the deserts," and it adds that "there remain now some 120 Armenian families in the town, consisting of mainly of children and elderly folk."

The focus on Sepastia also told the world that the heroic Armenians of Shabin Kara-Hissar and Amasia, exasperated at the savagery of the Turks took to reprisals, but were overwhelmed by large Turkish forces—and "died fighting to the last." Then to read the chilling account how about 15,000 Armenians of Erzinjan and its surrounding districts were for the most part "drowned in the Euphrates River near the Kamakh gorge."

I also pondered how I would survive the drive through the now barren, depopulated Armenian districts in eastern Turkey's Anatolian region. But I knew better. Nothing must interfere in my mission. I even kept my copy of the British Bluebook in my travel case; concerned the Turks would confiscate it on grounds it falsely condemned Ottoman Turkey of crimes against humanity. In present-day Turkey to even write about the Armenian genocide is seen as a crime against the Turkish state.

I also reminded myself to say a prayer for Surpouhi and Satenig, two young mothers from the village of Ketcheurd, just east of Sepastia. The two had thrown themselves in the Halys River, and were "drowned with their infants in their arms."

The two Armenian women chose death over life in a Turkish harem.

Then there was Surpouhi, the 19-year-old daughter of Garabed Tufenkjian of Herag. The Bluebook reported how she too died a horrible death, along with 17 other Armenian girls who had refused conversion to the faith of Islam and marriage to Turks. They perished near the Tshamli-Bel gorge.

I know it will get worse as we go further into the old Armenian provinces, and the descriptive account of what happened in 1915 is spelled out by the British Bluebook, which also contains maps of the towns and villages that bore the brunt of Ottoman Turkey's plan to exterminate the Armenian race.

The State Department airgram, in advising the U.S. Embassy in Adana of my mission, states clearly that I intend "to visit various cities in Eastern Turkey "once heavily populated by Armenians."

While there are some who question why we Armenians, years after the genocide of our people, still seek justice by forcing present-day Turks to pay the price for crimes committed by their forefathers, the present Turkish government denies the massacres ever took place. By refusing to face the truth of an evil past, the crimes of the past will cling to the Turkish nation and its people. By denial of the truth, justice remains denied.

Armenia's history is about a people that dates back into time, and a cause championed by the president of the United States who led our nation through World War I. I now pray for the souls of my people—and the young women of Sepastia region who paid the supreme sacrifice. But for now, my thoughts must remain with me. My Turkish guide and Kurdish driver are also at risk for taking an Armenian into the interior. I pray that no harm comes in our path.

On the advice of Mehmet, our excursion into the interior would follow the northern route. Though this travel plan would delay my arrival to the village of Kutluja, my two companions said it was the only way to see some of the historic Armenian villages and cities. I accepted their suggestion and we took the road to Amasia.

Before we take that journey into the Armenian Plateau, let me share with you some highlights on the history of the Armenian people in this and the following chapters.

During the ravages of World War I, and at the height of the infamous Turkish plan of genocide, thousands of school children in America responded to a universal plea heard around the world. The plea was "Help the Starving Armenians." The children of America, from Kansas to New York, came forth with their pennies and nickels and they asked: "Who are the Armenians?"

President Woodrow Wilson, a dedicated champion for Armenian justice and statehood had set aside two days in October, 1916 for America to open her heart to help the starving Armenians in a nationwide relief drive.

The heart of young America responded to the call of the destitute Armenian, once a proud Biblical race that now gasped with each breath for life in the forced exodus out of their ancestral homeland and into the torrid, desolate Syrian desert of Der el Zor.

Jacques de Morgan's "History of the Armenian People" is must reading for Armenians and persons who want to know how my people established their first political state. Armenian tradition tells us that an Armenian warrior named Haik, a great grandson of the legendary Noah, founded the first Armenian state in the Valley of Ararat—more than 2,000 years before the birth of Christ. The Armenian historian, Moses of Khoren, wanted, as did the early Armenian Christian missionaries—to link the birth of Armenia to Haik and thus to Noah and the Scriptures.

Moses and his counterpart historians have written that in the year 2,350 B.C., the warrior Haik defeated the armies of Belus the Babylonian to wrestle control of the regions of Erzurum and Van for his flock of followers. The Armenian scribes also write that the Indo-European Armenian left Thrace, crossed the Bosporous, fought and integrated with the then declining Hittite nation, later ventured into the lands of Cappadocia and finally settled upon the Valley of Ararat. It was at this point in time, and supported by modern-day Soviet Armenian historians, that the forming of the true Armenian nation came into being.

When the wandering Indo-European Armenian tribes settled upon the Valley of Ararat in their eastward march, they had entered the ancient state of Urartu and the two became one nation. The union, or marriage between the two Armenian tribes came with little difficulty. The once powerful Urartu nation had been weakened in its series of wars with the Assyrians, the Scythians and the Medes. The Urartu nation could not stop the Phrygian-bred Armenian, and the two merged with little killing and bloodshed. Haik's dark, stocky Armenian; and the tall blue-eyed light skinned Urartuans attained political identity for the new Armenian nation as early as the Sixth Century B.C.

Armenian history and its early beginning is a difficult task to substantiate. In present-day Soviet Armenia great advances are being accomplished to formulate a universal accepted look at the birth of the

Armenian people and their nation. In my search for the truth, or as close as one could get, I read about my people by reading the histories of the Assyrians, the Greeks, the Romans, the Persians, the Medes, the Parthians, the Urartuans, the Tatars, the Russians and by visiting with Soviet Armenian scholars. While much of Armenia's past is woven into the histories of other peoples, and their conquered past—much to my surprise, the history of my people is as accurate as any other people. Even in the writings of Herodotus, Strabo and Xenophon one will find reference to the Armenians of Ararat.

The term Armenia comes from the Persian inscriptions depicting the bloody battles between Darius and the Armenians as early as 520 B.C. The Greek historian Xenophon in 400 B.C. writes about his dealings with the Armenian kings during the retreat of a Grecian force of 10,000 through the highlands of Armenia. Historian-geographer Strabo writes about the Armenian language spoken by the inhabitants of the Ararat Region in the Second Century B.C. Still further, we read that in 190 B.C. when Antiochus the Great was defeated by Scipio, the Armenians seized upon the opportunity to rebel under the standards of one Artaxias to proclaim an independent kingdom. It was Artaxias who gave refuge to the exiled Hannibal.

Turning to the Book of Genesis, we learn that "...the Ark came to rest on the mountains of Ararat" and in Chapter IV of the Antiquities of the Jews, it states: "There is above the country of Minyas in Armenia a great mountain called Baris, as the story goes, many refugees sought safety at the time of the flood..."

In my travels about the nation, lecturing and sharing slides that depict barren depopulated historical Armenia, my audiences are awed at the beauty of majestic Mt. Ararat—and for many, they learn for the first time that Ararat was the landing site for Biblical Noah's Ark. Though the towering mountain of hope now rests within Turkey along the Soviet Armenian border, the Biblical mountain is embossed into the official coat-of-arms of the Armenian Soviet Socialist Republic. When the Turks protested to Moscow for allowing the Armenians to use Ararat in their national flag, the Russians responded: "And what right do you have to print a portion of the moon on the flag of Turkey." The

Turks stalked angrily away—my Yerevan-born Armenian writer friend Barkev Mardirosian always repeats with gusto.

While on a visit to the museum of Holy Etchmiadzin in Soviet Armenia, the churchmen showed me a gold container. In the container is a piece of darkened wood which the church professes to be from Noah's Ark.

Much of my knowledge on my Armenian heritage comes from the many sources I have outlined, and pieced together with my own personal opinion. If any one writer has truly opened my eyes into my heritage, and the tragedy of my people, it must be Arnold Toynbee in 'Murder of a Nation.' Yet I must not discount the writings of Franz Werfel in the 'Forty Days of Musa Dagh,' nor Jacques de Morgan's works—and of course my Armenian brothers at the State Historical Museum of Soviet Armenia. To these noble men of history, I am indebted. By profession I am a newspaper journalist. I make no claim at being a historian. I write what I see and hear and what I believe to be the truth. This is my attempt, and with your consent, we will take a look at the past of my people the Armenians.

It is said that in 538 B.C. the Armenian king, Tigranes the First had allied himself with Cyrus the Great in the destruction of the ancient city of Babylon—resulting in freedom for the enslaved Jews and the ending of 70 years of captivity by the Babylonians. Prophet Jeremiah, long before Babylon was destroyed, had proclaimed: "Call together against her kingdoms of Ararat, Minni, and Ashkenaz to make the land of Babylon a desolation without an inhabitant."

Then we come across the mention of Armenia in the inscriptions of Darius the First in 520 B.C. In which Darius describes the bloody battles his armies fought against "Arminya" in the Valley of Ararat. Armenians call themselves "Hyes" and their country "Hayastan."

The chains of Persian control over the Armenian Plateau were broken in the latter part of the Fourth Century B.C. with the eastern thrust of Alexander's Grecian-Macedonian armies. For the Armenian people, Alexander's reign brought culture, the development of cities and Hellenic architecture—which remains visible to this day in modern day architecture. But this golden age of Grecian culture in Armenia was short-lived. The legions of Rome were now on the horizon, and a new era was in the making for the Indo-European Armenian. Armenia had reached its peak as a military giant before the Romans swept them aside.

Tigranes the II was a young military genius. With his expertise he united the two separate Armenian kingdoms. He was destined to be Armenia's Caesar and Alexander—even if for a short time in history. Tigranes' conquests stretched from the Caspian Sea to the kingdom of Pontus on the Black Sea and southward to Syria and Israel along the eastern waters of the Mediterranean Sea. He was crowned King of Kings (94-54 B.C.)

Years later the Roman Senate struck coins in his honor. But before the honors of a coin struck in his honor, the Romans decided the adventurous Armenian king must be stopped.

For the Roman Senate, Tigranes was a living and viable threat to her holdings in western Asia Minor. Concern spiraled when news reached Rome that this upstart Armenian king had taken the Syrian city of Antioch and had turned his attention to the very gates of Israel. With the fall of Syria, Tigranes now ruled over 12 kingdoms. He rebuffed the threat from Rome and served notice he would retreat for no European empire. But in his response to Rome's call to back-off, Tigranes failed to heed another threat—the growing Parthian dynasty to the south. Now Rome was furious. The Senate dispatched the able Lucullus to teach the Armenian a lesson. Lucullus' eye was at the newly built city of Tigranocerta, a city Tigranes had constructed in his honor on the banks of the Tigris—and with the muscle of captive Greeks. When the two armies locked horns on the banks of the Tigris, Tigranes learned quickly his army was no match for the swift Romans. Tigranes was beaten. His army sent reeling into retreat, Tigranes headed for the mountains of the Armenian highlands. The over anxious Lucullus gave pursuit. But the Roman general failed to take into account that winter was setting in— and his army was headed for a disastrous expedition into the heartland of Armenia. Instead of victory, Lucullus returned to Rome in disgrace. The Armenian had outwitted him with a vanquished army. The Armenian winter saved Tigranes from total defeat.

On Lucullus' return to Rome, without Tigranes' crown, the infuriated Senate called upon Pompey to complete the task. When Tigranes learned of a second Roman attack, he appealed to his Asian friends to join in the war against Pompey and Rome. All responded but Parthia who had plans of her own. When the fighting began, Tigranes and his Asian legions stood their ground against Pompey. But the line of defense collapsed when Parthian troops entered Armenian territory. Suddenly Tigranes found he was alone. He had been deserted by his Asian allies.

Sensing certain doom for his people, Tigranes decided Armenia's destiny would be better served with the legions from Europe; rather than submit to her former Asian friends and Parthia. The once proud king rode into Pompey's camp to surrender his standards and crown to Rome. To Pompey's amazement, the Armenian king had not bowed for personal leniency but asked that his people be spared and called on Rome to evict Parthia from the Armenian Plateau. Pompey was impressed. He returned the crown to Tigranes and said, "You are a true king. Even in defeat you face your conqueror. Not to save your life but the lives of your people. Rome needs you."

In my readings about Tigranes I too have come to marvel this military giant in Armenian history. So impressed was I that to this day I carry a replica of a Roman coin struck in honor of Tigranes the Great. Though forced to relinquish control over Syria, Phoenicia, Cilicia, Pontus, Cappadocia, Gordyene, Sophene, Georgia and Azerbaijan, Tigranes saved Armenia. By decree, the Roman Senate restored Tigranes to royalty and as a show of trust, returned the lands of Gordyene (Kurdistan) and northern Mesopotamia to Armenia. In return, Tigranes and Armenia would be part of the Roman Empire—or to put it bluntly, the buffer state between east and west.

Why do I marvel Tigranes' diplomatic move to Rome? Simply, it linked pre-Biblical Armenia to Europe. It saved Armenia from gradual evaporation from the scene as a nation. Tigranes made the right decision. He lost the war but he won for future generations of Armenians.

Yet, before the eventual decline of Rome and Parthia, Armenia was turned into a sprawling battlefield. It was east versus west and Armenia right in the middle. In its wake, ruin and destruction of a glorious Hellenic civilization implanted by Alexander the Great. Soon after Tigranes' death, came the death of Armenia as a military power. To this very day, be it in present day Armenia, an Armenian community in Lebanon, Syria, France, South America, Canada, the United States or Romania, students of Armenian history remember the glory that was Tigranes the Great.

Down through the years that followed no other Armenian was able to marshal the forces as Tigranes had to strike the standard for one nation, one kind. Because of Armenia's inability to survive as a viable state for any given time, Tigranes was denied a niche in the world history books for his military conquests. To the Armenians Tigranes was a King of Kings.

After Tigranes' demise and the fall of Roman and Parthian influence in the Asia Minor peninsula the Armenians were to bow before the hoof beats of Sassanians, the Arabs, Tamerlane and his Tartars, Genghis Khan, the Byzantines, the Mamelukes of Egypt, the Persians and the Russians. Even the legions of Mark Anthony and Cleopatra struck terror into the Valley of Ararat. The worst was yet to come from the plains of Central Asia. They called themselves the Seljuk and Osmanli Turks.

The last Armenian kingdom, defined as Cilicia or Lesser Armenia, was within the southern region of Tigranes' old empire—along the shores of the Mediterranean with Adana as its seaport to the world.

The history of Cilicia Armenia is closely linked to the time of the Crusaders who set out to free the Holy Land. Because Cilician Armenians aided the Crusaders and offered comfort to Europe's warriors, Genghis Khan and the Mamelukes of Egypt were bent on teaching the Christian Armenians a lesson for all mankind to witness. After a series of attacks, the Armenian King Levon bowed before the Egyptian hordes from the south. In the year 1375 A.D. the last kingdom of Armenia succumbed. The Armenian king was taken to Cairo for public display—in chains.

When word spread through Europe that the Armenian king had been take captive the ambassadors and kings of Europe made repeated attempts to free King Levon at any price. Finally with the help of the Spanish Court, King Levon was set free on October 7, 1381. He spent the remaining days of his life living in exile as a guest of the church and state in France. This epitaph appears on the king's tombstone in Paris: "Here lieth the very noble and excellent prince Lyon the Fifth of Lizingue (Lusign) Latin King of the Kingdom of Armenia whose soul departed to God on the 29th day of November in the year of grace 1392. Pray for him."

In tribute to the Cilician Armenians Pope Gregory XIII in 1384 said in a Vatical decree: "Among the other merits the Armenian nation as regards the church and Christendom, there is one that is outstanding and deserves particularly to be remembered, namely, that when in times past the Christian princes and armies went forth to recover the Holy Land, no nation, no people came to their aid more speedily and with more enthusiasm than the Armenians."

One may ask at this point in Armenian history why the Armenians, surrounded in a sea of Islam, turned to the Christian doctrine even at the risk of banishment from their homeland. The Armenian Church is the oldest of all national churches. The Apostles Thaddeus and Bartholomew preached in Armenia, yet it was St. Gregory the Illuminator who won over the rulers of Armenia to the teachings of Christ. The Armenian Church dates back to 301 A.D. when King Tiridates the Third proclaimed that Christianity become the official religion of his nation; thus placing a niche in history as ruler of the first Christian state in the world.

At the Holy Etchmiadzin See in Armenia, tourists are told the story of Armenia's acceptance of Jesus' teachings. According to the church legend, King Tiridates had taken a serious illness. In a dream an angel told the ailing king he could be cured if he set St. Gregory free from a dungeon pit he had been sentenced. That morning after the harrowing dream the king inquired about the fate of St. Gregory. When told, he himself had St. Gregory sentenced to the pit 13 years ago he insisted the palace guards go to the pit and "bring St. Gregory to me." The guards tried to explain that when St. Gregory was thrown into the pit it had been filled with poisonous snakes and that no human being could have survived the snakes let alone thirteen years in a dungeon pit. When the guards went to the pit, shock set in. St. Gregory was alive—after thirteen years.

St. Gregory cured the ailing king and Christianity became the form of worship in Armenia. To this very day the story of St. Gregory's survival in a dungeon pit filled with snakes for thirteen years is repeated time after time.

In tribute to the Armenian saint and more than 1,600 years after the birth of the Christian state of Armenia a statue of St. Gregory the Illuminator was unveiled in 1974 at the Washington National Cathedral in Washington, D.C. The statue of St. Gregory was built on orders of the Very Rev. Francis B. Sayre Jr., Dean of the Cathedral. Rev. Sayre is the grandson of President Wilson. Truly a bond for justice that years later, Wilson's grandson, a ranking churchman in the nation's capital, was instrumental in paying honor to St. Gregory the Illuminator, the evangelist who spread the word of Jesus in Armenia: the land of Noah's Ark.

Another facet that binds the Armenian people is the language and alphabet of the Armenian—a member of the family of Indo-European languages. Though the language spoken in the Valley of Ararat was Armenian, the Armenians had no alphabet of their own. In 396 A.D. the scholarly apostle St. Mesrop Mashtotz gave the Armenians a unique alphabet unlike any other scripture. The scholars claim, or they would want us to believe, that had Armenia's church leaders not broken away from the grip of the Roman Catholic Church or the Greek Orthodox; and had the Armenians adopted the Latin alphabet instead of St. Mesrop's script, Armenia may have survived as a political state. In their thinking they failed to grasp the meaning of Armenianism—it includes the Armenian church and St. Mesrop's alphabet. The two kept the Armenians as one nation and they survived as "Giants of the Earth."

Who are the Armenians? They are an ancient people who founded a nation in the Valley of Ararat, and through the centuries were denied the right to guide and govern their own destiny. They boast their church is the oldest Christian state church in the world; even before Constantine decreed it for Rome in 307 A.D. Though they grieve over the near extermination of their people in Turkish-held Armenia, the Armenians, wherever they live, rejoice that in a small fragment of their ancestral homeland called present-day Soviet Armenia, the spirit of Sardarabad remains firm and with conviction.

These are the Armenians school children across America aided with their pennies and nickels in 1915. The "starving Armenians" starve no more. The tree of Armenia is growing again in the shadows of towering Mt. Ararat; in a small patch of land the Armenians call Mayr Hayastan (Mother Armenia)...

While the Jewish Holocaust and the Armenian Genocide remain as blots against humankind, we must remember that the Ottoman Turkish rulers carried out their genocidal execution on the historical homeland of the Armenian people.

That's why we can not forget.

CHAPTER FIVE

The history of the Armenian people has been marked by pain and suffering, but as William Saroyan etched in his Armenian manifesto, "you can burn their homes and churches but not their will to survive as a people."

Yet as we headed eastward my thoughts were about my Armenian friends in Detroit who also traced their roots to historical Armenia and the 1915 genocide—and how the four Armenian churches conduct special remembrance services on April 24th of each year to honor the memory of the more than one million who perished in 1915-23.

Whether you attend a remembrance service at St. John, St. Sarkis, Armenian Congregational or St. Vartan's Catholic Church, the services appeal for justice for the massacred Armenians. Within each Armenian Church community, the remaining genocide survivors still mourn for their fallen people—their sisters and mothers who were raped and violated before death.

The British Bluebook in graphic terms reported how "the women of Malatya were stripped naked and driven out from their homes, amid the gibes and jeers of the Muslim rabble. Many young women actually went mad; others resorted to hideously painful means to put an end to their lives." My friend Paul Kulhanjian, a Detroit public school educator, always speaks with pride that his roots can be traced to Malatya and he remains dedicated to seek justice for the soul of the massacred Armenians of ancient Malatya. "The Turks must pay for their crimes. What happened in 1915 is not ancient history. The Armenian genocide should be taught in our public schools, and we need people in Congress who will not let the Turk rewrite history at the expense of the Armenian people."

Paul is not alone at seeking justice for the rape and murder of his people.

Yet now the terrain ahead of us looked peaceful, though desolate. As I said earlier, pain and suffering has been one of the cruelties of being an Armenian. There have been some bright snapshots to Armenia's history. Like in the ninth century when a new age came to dawn in Armenia—the Arabs had been driven from the lands of Ararat.

The Armenian Bagratuni kings had established economic and cultural order within their domain and during this Golden Age in Armenia...impetus to architecture was the decree of the kings.

But the Armenians still lacked total self-determination. The Byzantine liberators of Armenia decided to stay on as protectorate of their Christian brothers claiming their presence would ward off further Arab raids into the heartland of Asia Minor.

As the turn of the century approached Turkish nomads began to infiltrate the Armenian Plateau. They came by the thousands having been forced out of their original nesting sites in central Asia's Turkestan with the Mongols in close pursuit. At first the intruding Turkish nomads appeared to be a peaceful lot of people who only sought the opportunity to live in peace. That mood was short lived.

By 1048 A.D. Turkish warriors began to sack low-land Armenian villages. The dark clouds of Turkish tyranny were now descending on Armenia. The armed Turkish intrusion of Armenia and the plains of Asia Minor failed to arouse the sleeping Byzantine rulers sitting in far off Constantinople—partly because of the Christian creed's separation of the Armenian and Byzantine churches in 451 A.D. at the Council of Chalcedon.

The Turks through contact with the Arabs had adopted the faith of Islam. Though the Turks had retained their Turkic language spoken on the plains of Central Asia, the advancing Turkish nomads adopted the Arabic alphabet which continued until Kemal Ataturk instituted the Latin alphabet to replace use of Arabic in Turkish life.

Of the ten various Turkish tribes, the Seljuks were at first the more domineering. In their quest to further the Turkic advance, Armenia was selected as the victim.

The first major Armenian community to fall before the invading Seljuk Turks was the majestic holy city of Ani—a city of churches. Next, the ancient fortress city of Kars bowed to Alp Arslan and his conquering Seljuks. Even then the Armenian plea to stem the Turkic advance fell on deaf ears in Constantinople. With the loss of Ani, the Armenian city of churches and the fortress at Kars—the conquest of Armenia and the Anatolian Plain was now in the making. But the biggest blow to Armenia's freedom was yet to come.

The year was 1071. The scene was Manzikert, an old Armenian settlement north of Lake Van. The Byzantine rulers had dispatched troops to Manzikert but help came too late. There the Seljuk leader Arslan crushed the Byzantine-Armenian armies of Romanus IV and the whole of Asia Minor was now at the mercy of the rampaging, victorious Turks. Had the Byzantine rulers heeded the earlier calls for help from their subject Armenians, the tide could have changed at Manzikert and the Turkish threat minimized.

The looting and killing that followed Arslan's sweep through Armenia is handed down to us by an 11th century Armenian chronicler, Aristaces of Lastivert. Historian Jacques de Morgan's priceless scholarly research repeats the writings of the Armenian chronicler, graphically: "Our cities were devastated, our homes and palaces burned, our royal halls reduced to ashes. Men were cut to pieces in the streets and women snatched from the homes. Infants were crushed on the pavements and the faces of young disfigured; maidens were ravished in the squares and youth killed in the presence of the aged; the heads of the old men were steeped in blood and their bodies rolled in the dust."

Never before had the Armenians encountered such savagery as experienced at the hand of the bloody Turks. Adding to this devastating blow came crippling raids by hordes of Tatars, Kurds and Mongolians. By the 11th century Armenia lost self rule and statehood. Yet the spirited Armenian found new hope on the northeastern shores of the Mediterranean for there the Armenians established the Cilician kingdom—a principality that became the new cradle of freedom for the children of the Valley of Ararat. This new found cradle of peace for the Armenian was short lived. In 1375 A.D. the last Armenian kingdom vanished under the hoofs of the invading Mamelukes of Egypt and the Armenian Plateau cried out in agony.

Meanwhile, the Seljuks began to lose their holdings in Asia Minor to the growing Persian dynasty—and the object of their battles was over the heartland of Armenia in the region of Lake Van. But a new kind of Turkish leadership was on the horizon. It was a devastating leadership that eventually gained a foothold in Europe for the Asian-bred Turkish nomad.

The new leader of the Turkish movement on the plains of Anatolia was a chieftain by the name of Ertughrul who founded the Ottoman Turk Federation. The term Ottoman came from his son Osman. By 1345 the Ottoman Turks had crossed the Dardanelles and all who waged combat with the Ottomans fell by the wayside including the decaying Byzantine Greeks and Seljuks. In due time the standards of the Ottomans then struck terror into Eastern Europe's Balkan States. The major prize in the Ottoman thrust into Europe came in 1453 with the fall of Constantinople and Ottoman Sultan Mohammed II renamed this majestic Greek city Istanbul.

While the Ottoman Turks knifed deeper into the Balkans, they kept a relentless watch on the southern flank of occupied Armenia. The Persian threat to Turkey's mounting war machine was real. The superior Ottomans drove the Persians out of southern Armenia by 1604 but not before the retreating Persians, under the command of Shah Abbas, set fire to the countryside and took hundreds upon thousands of Armenian slaves back to Persia. To this very day a large Armenian community continues in Persia, now known as Iran. It should be said that the Armenians of present day Iran have equal rights, schools and churches—and are held in high esteem by the Shah of Iran, but he is also hated by his own people as a tyrant dictator and a puppet for the U.S. State Department—a man who imprisons and tortures Iranian dissidents who oppose his dictatorial iron fist.

The years that followed the Turkish-Persian quest over Armenia offered no hope of respite and peace to the downtrodden Armenian. Even with the advent of Russian power into the Caucasus, little relief came to the Armenian. Continually the Armenian paid the supreme sacrifice only to be denied self-determination by her so-called liberators. Armenian scholars admit that had not Russian influence spread in the Caucuses Mountain range, Armenia would have surely died.

The renowned Soviet Armenian writer, Khachatur Abovian, while commenting on the liberation of that small sector of eastern Armenia and the removal of oppressive Persian tyranny said, "Blessed by the hour the Russian set his blessed foot on the sunny land of the Armenians and drove out the cursed evil breath of the Persians from our country." While glorifying the Russian the Armenian writer failed to dwell on the historical fact that colonialism continued to prevail in eastern Armenia. The Russian Imperial Army, on orders of Czar Nicholas, had no intention of granting complete freedom to the Armenian. But at least the presence of armed Russian troops would serve as a warning to the envious and suspicious Turks.

While the Armenian living in eastern Armenia with the protection of the Russian army enjoyed life the fate of the vast majority of the Armenian people imprisoned in western Armenia under the Ottomans remained unresolved.

The desire for a better life in western Armenia was evidenced in 1862 at the mountain village of Zeitun. The Armenians of Zeitun, an inland region of the Taurus Mountains of the once proud Cilician Armenian kingdom, had been able to retain a quasi-independent state even in the face of the superior numerical Ottomans. But in the summer of 1862 the Ottoman Turkish government decided it was time to crush this mountain stronghold. A Turkish army of great numbers set out for Zeitun. Repeatedly the men and women of Zeitun repulsed the Turkish army. Soon their heroic stand for freedom triggered other stands for freedom in western Armenia. As Armenians waged battles for justice they sang the patriotic songs of Zeitun—written in a revolutionary tone and spirit.

Less than 15 years after the epic defense for freedom at Zeitun a new hope appeared for the weary western Armenian. Turkey and Russia were at war. The hope was heightened when news reached the heartland of the mountain country that Russian backed Armenian volunteers had entered the ancient fortress city of Kars.

Before the Armenian volunteers could liberate their enslaved brothers in the dense Armenian sectors of western—held Armenia the Russians and Turks came to the peace table. Though saddened the Armenian found hope for reform when one of the conditions for peace was a proviso agreed upon at San Stefano that the Russians would have a hand at guaranteeing reform for the Armenians.

Reform never came to the Armenian. Envious international politics doomed the Armenian. The European powers of that time, leery of Russian influence in Ottoman Turkey, drafted another so-called reform plan at the Congress of Berlin held in the month of June 1878. Article 61 of the Congress called upon Turkey to carry out reform in the Armenian districts without Armenian or Russian intervention.

Further insult came when the Congress refused to allow the Armenian delegation a right to sit at the bargaining table. In essence, the powers to be told the Armenian Church leader Khrimian Hairig to take his flock back to Armenia. The spiritual leader of the Armenian Church wept in open as the heartless Europeans slammed the door on Armenia's claim to basic human rights. While a few voices spoke out for the Armenian Question, the blood-thirsty Sultan Abdul Hamid of Turkey was busy drafting his plan of reform for the Christian Armenians. Infuriated that the Armenian demand for reform got to the European scene, the Sultan, in 1894, put into operation a plan of an "Armenia without Armenians." Convinced the powers of Europe would not intervene the Sultan engineered the first stage of genocide against the Armenians. By 1896 more than 300,000 Armenians had been massacred.

But word of the Sultan's plan of genocide reached the capitals of Europe through the heroic efforts of English and American missionaries who risked certain death by daring to crack the Sultan's censorship of all mails leaving Turkey. Soon the conscience of the

Christian world was at stake. Finally, under the threat of risking intervention from Europe, Abdul Hamid cut short his plan of total extermination.

As barbaric were the conditions in my ancestral homeland in 1894-1896 the blood that spilled at the wish of Abdul Hamid was soon to be swamped by the monstrous crime that would follow in the spring of 1915. For his act of genocide Abdul Hamid earned the title of "Sick Man of Europe."

For the first time justice seeking peoples of the world were reading about the pre-Biblical Armenians. They were reading about the massacres in a highly documented report titled "Armenian Massacres and Turkish Tyranny" published in 1896. Yet unknown to authors Frederick Davis Greene, secretary of the National Relief Committee and Henry Davenport Northrop, a well known writer of his time, the darkest page in Armenian history was still to be written.

The date was April 24, 1915. The orders had been dispatched to Turkish officers in the interior of Armenia. The orders called for the total extermination of the Armenian race. No one was to be spared. The treacherous Young Turk movement, which earlier had promised reform to their Armenian subjects, had been ditched. These same Young Turks, who deposed Abdul Hamid, were bent on swinging the final blow to finish what the Sultan had started. In two short years the Ottoman Turkish government had put the sword to nearly two million Armenians. Those who survived in the highlands of Armenia died on the parched deserts of Syrian in what we Armenians call the "Second Exodus…"

In 1981 David Marshall Lang, the distinguished professor of Caucasian Studies at the University of London, was emphatic in condemning Ottoman Turkey for having committed genocide. Lang's chilling scholarly effort, "The Armenians, A People in Exile," said "the Armenian genocide was planned by the Young Turk junta well before the outbreak of the First World War is shown by the skillfully laid plans for the scheme and its lightning executions." He goes on to write that "the essence of the plan was secrecy. Since many telegraph operators, cipher clerks and local government officials were themselves Armenian, care was taken to avoid putting detailed instructions on paper. In many cases the extermination scheme was put into operation on receipt of the simple message: "Take care of the Armenians." He repeats the telegraphed message of September 15, 1915 to the Governor of Aleppo, from Minister of Interior Talaat Pasha ordering the extermination of "all the Armenians living in Turkey" while emphasizing +"Their existence must be terminated." One may ask "How could the Turks have killed nearly two million Armenians in eight years" and further question that similar holocausts can be found in the dark pages of man's inhumanity to man…"

In the beginning the Turks removed the threat of a fighting male Armenian population by recruiting nearly 200,000 men between the ages of 18 and 50 on the pretense they would serve in the Turkish military. Instead group by group the 200,000 Armenian male force was annihilated. Then they came after the old men, the women and the children. The destination was certain death—the hot sands of the Der el Zor desert of Syria awaited the uprooted Armenians. In this forced exodus nearly 1,500,000 men, women and children perished. By sheer miracle more than 500,000 Armenians survived to find refuge and life in Arab lands while less than 200,000 found their way to Russian occupied eastern Armenia.

At the turn of the century the Armenian populace in western held Turkish Armenia numbered nearly three million. Yet in the summer of 1969 as I retraced the steps of my ancestral past in Turkish held Armenia the Turkish Ministry of Tourism told me that no more than 50,000 known Armenians still live on the ancestral lands of their forefathers. In essence a whole nation succumbed to the loathsome Turkish plan of genocide. It was made possible because the world was at war and Turkey was free to rid herself of the Armenians. What crime did my people commit to suffer such a holocaust? If wanting basic human rights is a crime then the greater crime was Turkey's sadistic plan of extermination. During World War I Turkey had thrown her support with Kaiser Germany. But to all available information the Germans ignored the massacres in Turkey. During the height of the massacres in the region of Moush we are told that sympathetic German officers pleaded with the Turks "to save a few Armenians for the museums" as a ploy to get the Turks to stop the wanton killing.

Strange as it seems that 23 years after the genocide in Armenia another plan of genocide was taking shape in Europe. This time the victims were to be the defenseless Jewish and Polish people. Hitler's plan would claim the lives of six million innocent people. When questioned on August 22, 1939 about his plan of extermination with no mercy or pity of men, women and children the mad Nazi henchman uttered, "After all who remembers today the extermination of the Armenians."

Hitler and his Nazi madmen were eventually destroyed and brought to public trial by the free peoples of the world. Man still shudders over the barbaric horrors inflicted on six million European Jews and millions of Poles, Danes, French, Russians and others the Nazi region set out to exterminate.

The Turk still stalks the Armenian Plateau. She rules over a mass graveyard without having to stand trial at a Nuremburg type court. Turkey still gloats, while denying genocide took place. The Turkish government of today simply asks that the Armenian forget the past. How can we forget the first genocide of the 20th century? The genocide that Hitler copied in his plan to rid Europe of six million Jews.

While the Turk ignored the pleas of the Wilson's, the Gladstone's, the Bryce's and the Toynbee's so did Europe during the Second Genocide that brought death to six million Jews.

In 1967 Arthur D. Morse, the distinguished reporter-director for Edward R. Morrow's 'See It Now' television series, and a CBS producer, wrote a chronicle of American apathy in "While Six Million Died," In the chilling account, Morse repeated the plea for English intervention to save the Jews of Germany in which Sir Herbert Samuel, turned to his peers and declared, "This is not an occasion on which we are expressing sorrow or sympathy to sufferers from some terrible catastrophe due unavoidably to flood or earthquake or some other convulsion of nature. These dreadful events are an outcome of quite deliberate, planned, conscious cruelty of human beings. The only events even remotely parallel to this were the Armenian massacres of fifty years ago...they aroused the outspoken indignation of the whole of civilized mankind and they were one of the causes of the downfall of the Turkish empire."

We know well that the then sleeping world failed to heed the Briton's warning and as man became embroiled in the agony of World War II the Nazis were free to carry out their plan to exterminate.

For the European Jew death came at concentration camps that shocked mankind. For the Armenian the plan to exterminate came in a November 23, 1915 communiqué to the Turkish governor at Aleppo, Syria. It read: "Destroy by secret means the Armenians of the Eastern Provinces who pass into your hands there." This death note was signed by Talaat. Years after the collapse of the Ottoman Empire Turkish officials refuted the orders dispatched on the signature of Talaat. They said the death orders had been forged by anti-Turkish networks.

Years after the near extermination of the Armenian people Talaat met death on the streets of Berlin. An Armenian agent, Soghomon Tehrlirian, had avenged his people. After the internationally covered trial, Tehrlirian was released. A German jury found the Armenian innocent of the murder charge on grounds that the assassination of Talaat was justifiable homicide.

In earlier chapters we quoted from prominent men of history and those who held the highest offices in government. President Ford reaffirmed his condemnation of Turkey's genocide of the Armenian people and his successor to the White House, President Jimmy Carter shares the same condemnation. In addition to issuing a statement of the Armenian Question the 39th president of the United States of America makes strong reference to the genocide and that "the tragedy of history has not been corrected."

If the present day rulers of Turkey, a NATO ally of the United States and fellow United Nations member nation had hoped the change in command in the White House would be to their benefit, President Carter's position statement dealt the Turks another historical blow.

I would like to share with you some of the comments from Carter. "As leader of the Democratic Party, the party of Woodrow Wilson a man who showed compassion for the Armenian people at a time when they were subjected to extreme injustice, I will ensure that the voice of the Armenian people will be heard."

And like President Ford our new American president deals firmly with the question of genocide. His words of historical fact are: "An estimated one and a half million persons were murdered during this 'first genocide of the 20th century,' yet even though the tragedy of history has not been corrected, Armenians, wherever they are, continue to maintain their culture and strong desire for freedom. The time has come for the world to recognize that the use of genocide as a national policy by any nation is a crime against humanity which must be condemned."

The long road to justice is a painful journey but the Armenian will never cease in the quest for justice—nor will the men and women who serve the highest offices in this land and other freedom loving nations across the planet Earth.

It has been a long time since the era of Woodrow Wilson. The voices of justice did not die with that champion for Armenian justice. It still lives. Presidents Ford and Carter, by their noble gestures, have kept the cause alive and vibrant.

In the chapters that follow we will embark into the heartland of historical Armenia and together relive the agony of the first genocide of the 20th century.

Hopefully at the end of the journey we will find the strength to continue the march for justice. The justice I seek is in memory of my slain ancestors; uncles, aunts, grandparents, cousins—my people.

The distinguished elder English statesman, Prime Minister William Gladstone, said: "To serve Armenia is to serve civilization."

CHAPTER SIX

"Then all the men were taken, bound, and some of them killed between Amasia and Tokat. All those who reached Tokat were directed towards Tchiftlik or Gishgisha and murdered. The women and children were taken in ox-carts to Sharkisla; then they were taken to Malatya, and finally thrown into the Euphrates River," states the documented 1916 published British Bluebook—"The Treatment of Armenians in the Ottoman Empire."

Who were these Armenians destined to a fate of horrific deaths. They were the Armenians of Merzifon, Samsun, and Amasia—as reported in an August 26, 1915 report filed by the American Committee for Armenian and Syrian Relief. Some of the victims included the grandparents, aunts and uncles, cousins and classmates of my stepmother, Lucy Baronian Kehetian.

The ancient Asia Minor cities of Samsun, Amasia and Merzifon date back to the Byzantine Empire—and further into the time of Julius Caesar and Alexander the Great. For centuries the Greeks and Armenians lived in these cities. But as the advancing Turks penetrated the northwestern region of the Asia Minor scene, havoc and death followed the Seljuk and Ottoman Turks.

My original route called for a southerly drive to the old Armenian city of Sepastia, now known as Sivas by the Turks. But at the urging of my step-mother I promised to visit Merzifon, her birthplace. When we arrived in Merzifon, I was amazed at the beauty of the old Byzantine city. The Grecian architecture still prevailed in the city's old sections.

Before I left for my mission to Turkish-held Armenia and my search for Aunt Parancim, I called my step-mother at her home in Fresno,

California to assure that Merzifon was on my list of places to visit. You can well imagine the thrill in her voice when I revealed my journey plans included Merzifon. Lucy was in her third year of college in Merzifon when she was brought to Providence, Rhode Island to escape the wrath of the Turks. Two years after leaving Merzifon, Lucy and her parents learned the massacres had swept through the old city.

In recalling that dark day when she had to leave the homeland, Lucy wept as she shared her life story: "The Turks killed my two brothers for refusing to turn over the property deed of the family farm to the Turkish military. Because of their refusal, the Turks blamed my father. When they killed my brothers we knew my father would be next on their hate list." To escape a similar fate, Lucy, along with a sister and parents left for America on February 1, 1913 aboard a Greek liner out of the Black Sea port city of Samsun.

On leaving Merzifon, Lucy said: "Before we left, my father faithfully promised to send for the remaining Madaksian relatives once he was able to earn enough money in America. I still remember kissing my grandparents, my relatives, and classmates. They died during the massacres. All of them, no one survived."

The college Lucy attended was the old American Anatolian College in Merzifon—then a school with a large student enrollment of Greeks and Armenians. On July 21, 1969 I stood before the gates of the old school, but the voices of students were not heard. The old college had been converted into a military depot. It was now in dire need of repairs with broken windows, crumbling steps and litter in its courtyard. I was aghast at the condition of the old school. The Turks did not lift a finger to repair the old school.

Little did I know then the decay of Merzifon's past linkage to the Greeks and Armenians was nothing compared to what I would find in the interior of historical Armenia. I still recall that dreary November day in 1966 when we buried my father at the Armenian Ararat Cemetery in Fresno. Before leaving the cemetery, Lucy said: "Your father told me many times that you had vowed as a boy to one day visit his birthplace in Khoops and your mother's in Erzurum. If you can fulfill that pledge, please also honor your step-mother. Please go to Merzifon. Bring back the soil of Merzifon. When I die, sprinkle the earth of Merzifon on my grave."

Lucy's wish was fulfilled on May 8, 1976. When Lucy's remains were being lowered to her final resting place at Ararat Cemetery, I sprinkled the earth of Merzifon on her casket. Even in death the Armenian longs for the soil of the ancestral homeland. Some call us fanatical nationalists for our beliefs. Tell me is it wrong to love the earth that gave you life? Is it wrong to love the soil that a nation died for to preserve for future generations? The soil of Merzifon was dear to Lucy. May she now rest in eternal peace.

While I fulfilled my mission to Merzifon, Nur and Mehmet suggested we have lunch in the old city. "While you have lunch, I will inquire if any Armenians still live here," Nur added. Not too long after, Nur hurried back to the dirty, dingy restaurant. "I found an Armenian named Hagop. He runs an ice cream store down the street. He wants to meet you," my Turkish guide repeated.

As we walked swiftly to Hagop's confectionary, I thought of Lucy. What a stroke of good fortune if this Hagop knew Lucy and her family. As we approached the doorway, a tall slightly built man emerged. He was Hagop Gumus. His eyes sparkled when I greeted him in Armenian. Before another word was exchanged, Hagop appealed that I honor his house with a visit. "My family will be honored to welcome the first Armenian from America to our home and Merzifon." I was equally excited, and accepted Hagop's warm Armenian expression. He was the first Armenian I met since leaving Ankara, and my visit with Zadik the jeweler.

Once at Hagop's home, his children and grandchildren soon arrived. They wanted to meet the Armenian from America. Soon a few more Armenians arrived, as word spread through the community of nine Armenian families that Hagop had a visitor who was heading into historical Armenia. After explaining the purpose of my mission, Hagop and his wife wished me "God-speed in your mission," and urged I be cautious once in the interior. Hagop and his wife did not know Lucy or her family. "My wife and I were orphaned during the war. I wish we could help you, but we can not," Hagop apologized.

As we chatted about the lifestyle of Armenians in America and Soviet Armenia I detected some caution on part of the Gumus family. Though I still had some reservations on Nur's assignment to be my guide, I assured Hagop they could speak freely. Even though the attaché at Ambassador Handley's office strongly suggested I refrain from discussing the massacres with Armenians in Turkey.

Midway through the discussion, Hagop's wife asked if the Armenians of America still adhere to their Christian faith. I nodded yes, and told her we have four Armenian churches in Detroit. Pleased at my response, she then pointed to the crucifix on the living room wall. I did not have to ask. It was clear that this Armenian family was not intimidated by the Muslim Turks.

When I inquired about Armenian life in Merzifon, Hagop and his son Dikran said the few Armenians in their city were treated fairly by the Turks. Then the discussion turned to Soviet Armenia. "Our poor people must find it unbearable living under the Russians and communists. We always read in the papers about the dire conditions in Armenia and how our people suffer," Dikran stressed.

Now I had to speak. I wanted Hagop and the Armenians in his home to know life was improving in Soviet Armenia since the death of Josef Stalin, that the schools and universities in Yerevan were the best. I wanted them to know that the Russians support the Armenian people. I then told Hagop that Armenians from throughout the world can now visit Soviet Armenia as I did the previous year. The reaction was heartening. "You bring us good news about our people. God is answering the prayers of the Armenians," Mrs. Gumus voiced with pride

The smiles throughout the room even caught Nur's attention. He then asked: "You have made these people happy with your news. What did you say in Armenian?" I then repeated my commentary about life improving in Soviet Armenia, and how conditions were improving. Nur did not ask that I amplify my remarks about the slow, but gradual recovery of economic life in Soviet Armenia.

It was now time to bid farewell to Hagop, his family and friends who had gathered at his home to welcome me to Merzifon. As Hagop and I embraced before heading for Sepastia, we exchanged best wishes as Armenians do when parting after a happy occasion. Hagop then blessed me with a prayer. "Be careful my son. You are going to places we dare not venture. May the Almighty and St. Gregory protect you."

As Mehmet's Chevrolet inched away from the home of Hagop Gumus I glanced back for one final look…and in the dust that trailed, I saw an old man smiling. I had brought him good news that life is improving in Soviet Armenia, and that national pride is evident throughout the small country. I also fulfilled my pledge to my stepmother Lucy.

Our next stop was Amasia, a once majestic Grecian metropolis south of the Black Sea. In 1916, reports the British Bluebook, travelers reaching Samsun were telling a shocked world that "You can hardly find an Armenian left in Amasia…" We were in Amasia 53 years after the 1916 report spelled out in the Bluebook. We inquired on the whereabouts of Armenians in Amasia, only to learn there were no Armenians. A store-keeper told Nur that he heard that several Armenian women, married to Turks, were living in the nearby mountain villages. "But here in Amasia we have no Armenians. They left during the war," the store-keeper emphasized. Oh how I wanted to shout back they didn't die in a war, that the fucking Turks massacred them. But I kept my mouth shut.

Despite the absence of Armenians, I am glad we stopped in Amasia. This is a city that dates back to the time of the Hittites and Phrygians. It was here that the kings of ancient Pontus, longtime allies of pre-Biblical Armenia built their fortresses to stem the Roman advance into Asia Minor. History also tells us that in 63 B.C. the Greek geographer Strabo was born in Amasia. Turkish legend tells the story that the Greek and Armenian defenders fought for six months in defending the gateway into Amasia—but only to succumb when a light came from the heavens, a light that fell on the Seljuk warriors. With the fall of Amasia in 1075, the Seljuk Turks continued their westward march to Constantinople and Eastern Europe.

We were now back on the dusty dirt trail when I spotted a road sign pointing to a town called Zile. I motioned to Mehmet to follow the dirt road to Zile. Nur tried to change my request. "According to my map this small village is not worth going off our schedule," my young guide stressed. But I prevailed. I wanted to see Zile, for it was on the plains of Zile that Caesar pronounced "Veni, vidi, vici"—(I came, I saw, I conquered.) Instead of Roman legions going into combat, the fields of Zile now shifted with the breeze. Caesar echoed his historic phrase in 47 B.C. after defeating Pharnaces, the king of Pontus—so it is etched by Roman historians. Nur and Mehmet were not aware that Zile has its niche in Roman history.

The few hours we detoured to Zile were refreshing for me. For the first time since arriving in Turkey, my mind was on something unrelated to my mission to historical Turkish-held Armenia and my search for Aunt Parancim, my father's sister. It was historically refreshing, even for Nur.

We were now two hours out of Sepastia. The last town before reaching our destination for the day would be Tokat, a city once within the vast domain of Tigranes the Great, the Armenian king who in 55 B.C. dared to defy the Roman Empire. The Armenian influence in Tokat survived the Romans, Alexander, the Persians and the Byzantines. But the Armenian stronghold in Tokat died when the city was placed on Talaat Pasha's list for extermination. As was the case in Amasia, we could not find one single Armenian in Tokat. I didn't expect to after having read about Tokat's fate in the British Bluebook.

It was now nightfall. Mehmet strongly advised we proceed to Sepastia. "These roads are not safe for night driving, even for Turks," he voiced in Turkish and English. I agreed. In another hour or so we would be in Sepastia, once the most heavily populated Armenian community west of the Valley of Ararat. For Armenians who trace their roots to Sepastia, their pride is second to none. They'll correct those who use the Turkish name Sivas when talking about their Armenian ancestry from Sepastia.

As we entered the city, I felt inspired. For now I was within the historical land of my people. If Vahan Solakian and Harry Derderian were with me, my two Detroit friends would be beaming. Let me explain: Vahan is married to Rose's cousin, Alice Kachadourian, who always reminds her husband that it was the Armenian saint from Moush, St. Mesrop Mashtotz, who gave the Armenians an alphabet. "Yes, but it was the clever Armenian merchants of Sepastia who were envied by the business world," was Vahan's rapid response. He also reminded our circle of friends that the Armenian resistance hero, Mourad of Sepastia, who drove fear into the Turkish military, was "a proud Sepastatzi."

Harry was also a boasting Sepastatzi, who repeated after his marriage to Helen Baronian, who had family roots to the Keghi-Khoops district of historical Armenia. "Helen and I will make a great team. We both trace our roots to the heartland of Armenia—Sepastia and Keghi. . We'll have great children," my friend frequently lectured with a smile—during the coffee hour after Sunday services at the St. Sarkis Church where he served as a trustee on the church board.

But now the hour was late. I would take some pictures for Vahan and Harry in the morning. I know Harry would have some sharp words for the Turks who now run the city. "The bastard Turks committed genocide, and the world let them get away with the crime. A bystander to a crime is also a criminal," he pontificated at every opportune.

CHAPTER SEVEN

French literary great Victor Hugo said "The Turk has trodden on this land, all is in ruins."

Talaat Pasha's sinister edict to "destroy by secret means" was evident when I entered Sivas on the night of July 20, 1969—a city the Armenians call Sepastia. This historic town served as the western defense-line for the pre-Urartu Armenian civilization.

Prior to Talaat's 1915 genocide order, more than half of the city's population was Armenian. Now the Armenians number no more than 500 souls. Our late arrival into Sepastia ruled out any chance of searching out the remaining Armenians. Nur promised "the first task we face in the morning is to find you some Armenians."

Before retiring for the night in the only hotel in Sivas, I checked my notes on the history of this old Armenian city. I read the clip taken from a magazine of the National Geographic Society. The item was about Tamerlane's victory against the Seljuks at Ankara—and of his hate of Armenians. Shortly before his victory at Ankara, the Asian warrior had taken ill in the town of Hafik. He accused the Armenians of trying to poison him. In a state of anger Tamerlane ordered a heinous decree: "Bury the Armenians alive...let them die with their horses." When the Asian tyrant had finished, 4,000 Armenian cavalrymen had been buried alive—strapped to their dead horses. This tale of horror has been passed on from one generation to another, mostly by Kurdish nomads now occupying Hafik and other historical Armenian settlements. When the earth trembles in this region, the Kurds say it is caused by the restless souls of the Armenians and their horses. The Kurds even claim to have heard the pounding of hoof-beats and have seen rider-less horses in the cold of the night when the earth trembles.

Hafik is in the Anatolian fault...an earthquake belt stretching eastward to Erzurum and towering Mt. Ararat by the border to Soviet Armenia. But to the Kurdish nomads, scientific explanations have no rational value. They remain convinced the earth trembles because of the restless souls of the Armenians and their horses, slain and buried on Tamerlane's orders.

Just before I closed my eyes, there was a knock at the door. Nur had convinced the hotel chef to brew us some Turkish coffee. "I know you like coffee. We've had a busy day. Some Turkish-brewed coffee would hit the spot. I'll join you." In the café the manager of the Hotel Kosk asked if he could join us at our table. Wisely we extended the invite. With the hotel manager at our table, we were showered with some of the finest Turkish pastries. That's when I asked the manager about the "folk tale of Hafik." The friendly hotel manager laughed. "We Turks don't believe in such tales. The Kurds are a superstitious people. That's why we call them 'mountain Turks.' That folk tale story in the magazine comes from the Kurdish storytellers."

After my second cup of the thick coffee and pastries it was now past the midnight hour and time to retire. Nur also reminded me: "In the morning we will explore Sivas to find some Armenians."

Once in my room, I recorded the day's activities in my notebook before closing my eyes for what proved to be a restless sleep. Four hours later I sprung up from my bed. I could hear the hoof-beats of horses. I felt a cold chill, and immediately thought of the story in the National Geographic magazine—and the Kurds who swear by stories of the rider-less horses and the trembling earth. The beat of the hoofs grew louder by the second. I grasped for the tattered light string. You can imagine how foolish I felt. I could see the culprit was a leaky water faucet. I returned to my bed, though still shaken by my nightmare. Before too long I drifted back into a deep sleep, but without a shivering experience. I made sure the water faucet was secure. No more drip, drip, drip.

Three hours later a different sound aroused me. The clattering of morning traffic in the street below was loud. I pushed open my window to inhale the freshness of the early morning air. The street traffic flow had a touch of the traffic jams I would encounter in my morning commutes to work but from what I could observe from my window, the roadway was filled with slow-moving vehicles and farm trucks. People were milling about the entrance to the hotel. Yet all of the excitement below did not touch me. All I could see was a sea of Turks. I kept my cool. As a kid growing up in southwest Detroit, I learned to hate Turks. No one had to teach me to hate them. When I would ask my mother why didn't I have grandparents, aunts and uncles like my classmates at Cary School, I knew the answer: The Turks killed them. But I had a mission to fulfill, and I would settle my score with the Turk at another time. In looking back, my mother always taught me to be a proud American, and equally so a proud Armenian. When she would talk about her birth and early childhood life in Erzurum, my mother always emphasized the importance of heritage pride. From the day of my birth at the old Harper Hospital in Detroit, life was a constant struggle for my mother. The doctors said if she lived, my mother would never recover fully to enjoy a quality life. The medical assessment proved accurate.

My mother died at age 54. Most of her adult life after my birth was mere survival. Simply put, her life was shortened by refusing to abort my birth—and not because our laws at that time prohibited abortion. When I asked why she insisted at giving me life, when the doctors had warned that a fifth pregnancy would threaten her own quality of life, Mom's response was one I will treasure to my last breath. She wanted to give birth to a son to carry her father's name. When we get to Erzurum, I will offer a prayer to my mother for giving me life and the baptismal name of Moushegh—which was her father's name.

But for now the focus of my mission had brought me to historic Sepastia. After getting dressed, I proceeded to the hotel restaurant to have breakfast with Nur and Mehmet. My young Turkish guide had been up since the break of dawn inquiring about Armenians in Sivas. Nur was beaming: "Mr. Kehetian, today you will meet some

Armenians. The director of Sivas says there are more than 500 Armenians in this city. Some of them own linen and jewelry shops. We must find them before we leave this afternoon for the drive through the Manzur Mountains to Erzurum, your mother's birthplace.

Less than a block away from the hotel, we came upon Torkum's linen store. Torkum's hospitality was beautiful. He closed the store, suggesting: "This calls for a celebration. Wait till my friends meet you. I can not believe it. An Armenian from America is in our city." When we reached Torkum's friends, they too expressed Armenian pride. Manuk and Savak also closed their business, a jewelry store. Together, with Nur, we went to a coffee house and spent the next two hours talking about the fate of our people. My friends in Sivas were also pleased when I told them that my friends in America who trace their Armenian roots to this city, still call it Sepastia. "That's good. Armenians must never forget Sepastia."

I then told my new-found friends about the proud children of Sepastia back in Detroit. Like proud Sepastatzi Onnig Hachigian. My friend Onnig and I served with the same Armenian language interrogation unit for the U.S. Army Reserve Military Intelligence Organization. Onnig, a World War II veteran, was always writing letters to newspapers and members of Michigan's congressional delegation urging they support passage of the Armenian genocide resolution. He repeatedly lectured: "We must not stop in our demands for justice." Before I left for Turkey Onnig said: "You must go to Sepastia to spit in the eye of the Turk. Those bastards killed my people. Then you can say you saw the heartland of Armenia, and repeat a prayer for our massacred ancestors."

I know Onnig, along with Vahan and Harry will be enthused when I tell them about the three Armenians I visited with in Sepastia, and how dedicated my three "friends in Sepastia" are at preserving Armenia's identity in this old city. For Onnig, I also prayed for the nameless graves of Sepastia.

At this point Nur cut into the discussion I was having with Manuk, Savak and Torkum. "I don't understand Armenian, but the four of you greet each other like blood brothers. This is beautiful. I envy you."

I wanted to explain, but this was not the time. Whenever two Armenians meet, we reach out to each other. We do because we are the children of genocide survivors. A genocide the Turk rebuffs, claiming the number of slain Armenians was padded and that those who died were the victims of civil unrest and war. Shame on the Turk who believes that lie, and those who allow present-day Turkish leaders to blackmail U.S. presidents into reneging on their campaign pledges to address the genocide issue after getting into the White House.

My visit with Torkum, Manuk and Savak was electrifying. They told me how the Armenian parents of Sepastia work to send their sons and daughters to Istanbul "to attend Armenian schools to retain our faith and culture." May God grant them their wishes. Here we have a handful of Armenians left, the children of genocide survivors and they stand tall like true giants of the earth. They work to give their children a better life, a life with Armenians in Istanbul who have freedoms that are not possible to uphold in the interior of barren depopulated historical Armenia .

Manuk's eyes sparkled when I told him of my mission, my search for Aunt Parancim and the fulfillment of boyhood pledges to visit the birthplaces of my mother and father. "Go to Erzurum. Rekindle the spirit of your mother's heritage. But do not expect to find any Armenians there. We've been to Erzurum. The Armenians are gone. It was once a great Armenian community we were told, and they called the city Garin in Armenian.

Before it was time to depart, my three Armenian comrades of Sepastia took me to view the old Armenian section of the city. It was a sad picture to behold. Just slums now occupied by poverty-stricken Kurdish nomads. I wept looking out at the ghost of old Sepastia, and would have to share this scene with my Armenian friends back in Detroit who take pride at being "Sepastia Hyes," and jump with joy when the music at an Armenian party is a "Sepo" dance.

As I brushed away my tears, I wasn't alone. Torkum, Manuk and Savak were also misty-eyed. We embraced. Nur was watching. He knew we were experiencing a pain that had been triggered by our Armenian heritage and what was before us. Rows of shacks strung along a creek that had run dry from the intense July heat. Manuk then clutched my hand and openly prayed that "God protect this Armenian in search of his heritage and his father's sister, Parancim."

At that moment, as we exchanged parting hugs and prayers, I knew the Turkish plan to eradicate my people had failed.

My meeting with Torkum, Manuk and Savak was testimony to the spirit of the Armenian people. At no time did my three friends shy away from their Armenian roots, knowing we were being watched closely while we toured the old Armenian settlement. Now I can tell my friends in Detroit that the spirit of Sepastia still lives.

Back home in Detroit, my old pal since our teen years, Adam Manoogian, would have had some choice words for the Turks of Sepastia. His mother and father were survivors of the murder of Sepastia. When we'd attend an Armenian gathering, have a few drinks, our talk would then center on the massacres. Adam was blunt. He would say: "Do you realize more than one million of our people were massacred by the fucking Turks, and by some miracle our parents survived. Because of that miracle today we are friends. We must not forget the horrific price that was paid to make this happen. Our friendship was the result of a genocide. We must never forget. Promise me that my fellow Armenian brother."

We repeated our pledge of brotherhood in Ambridge, Pa., when Adam served as a member of the wedding party in my marriage to Rose Sarkisian.

The British Bluebook has scores and scores of pages devoted to the destruction of Sepastia. "In the town of Sivas itself, which comprised 25,000 Armenians, many of the important inhabitants have either been killed or deported to the deserts. There now remains 120 Armenian families in the town, consisting mainly children and elderly folk. The slaughter of Sivas also touched into the mountain villages nearby. At Maltepe, a village east of Sivas, 20 Armenians were hacked to pieces with pointed and spiked hatchets. At Duzasar the Armenians were done in the same manner—the Bluebook describes. And at Habesh, 3,800 Armenians were pole-axed, stoned or bayoneted

The British Bluebook also relates to the heroic stand taken by the Armenians of the mountain range of Shabin Kara-Hissar, just east of Sepastia. But I already knew the story. Harry Yangouyian never missed a chance to tell the story his father read to him as a youngster. "My ancestors fought for their freedom, and the Turks paid a heavy price to capture their mountain village. Some day we will avenge the massacres of our people, Harry would lecture when called to recite patriotic Armenian essays at the Armenian Community Center in Detroit. After the massacres, Harry's father was the sole survivor of the Yangouyian family.

I thought of Harry as we motored past the trail to the Eagle's Nest. The Bluebook tells the story: "Exasperated at the unaccountable savagery of the Turks, the Armenians took to reprisals. They burnt down the Muslim quarters and government buildings and temporarily drove the Turks from them. Later, however, they were overwhelmed by large Turkish forces, and died fighting to the last." Yet the day we drove past Shabin Kara-Hissar, the scene was quiet. I could hear nothing but the stillness of death. For out there on the mountains of that heroic village called the 'Eagle's Nest," Harry's ancestors fought to the bitter end for the right to live as a free people. No one came to their aid.

It was at this juncture that I grasped at what Talaat sought in the plan of genocide. By removing the two million Armenians in the eastern districts of Anatolia in the Ottoman Empire, through massacres and wholesale deportations, Turkey would be able to withstand any Armenian push for statehood and freedom if Ankara lost out by having joined in its alliance with Germany during World War I. When the western Allies defeated Germany and its partners in crime, Turkey did not have to worry about Armenian claims for statehood. Talaat had taken care of the Armenian Question by genocide. The wholesale extermination of the Christian Armenian populace by Muslim Turkey was not a clash between religious faiths. The plot was sinister and calculated to its fullest. It worked. When Woodrow Wilson drafted the boundaries for a new Armenia in 1920 for the League of Nations, the provinces of Wilson Armenia had been stripped of their Armenian settlements—like was experienced in Sepastia.

Yet I am told to forgive present-day Turkey because it had nothing to do with the genocide. That will never happen. The bastard government in Ankara remains corrupt by denying its past. How can I forgive the Turk when his government says there was no genocide, no wholesale massacre of the Armenian people on their ancestral homeland.

By now we were on the outskirts of Eagle's Nest headed for Erzinjan. The Bluebook tells me that Erzinjan, a mountain town, once boasted an Armenian community of 15,000 before the massacres of 1915-23. What happened to the Armenians of Erzinjan? Again a picture of death as reported in the Bluebook: "About 15,000 Armenians of Erzinjan and its surrounding villages were for the most part drowned in the Euphrates near Kamakh gorge. Our stay in Erzinjan was brief. We refreshed ourselves with the cool waters of Erzinjan's mountain springs. Soon the area's Kurds were upon us. They wanted to know who I was, where were we going. Nur was getting nervous. He told me to get back in the car, and urged Mehmet to get us back on the road. "Look, these are mountain people. They don't even care for Turks from Ankara. Let's get out of here."

I could go on and on to list similar experiences and stories of despair taken from the British Bluebook or Arnold Toynbee's "Murder of a Nation." But to remain silent is also a crime. If the question of genocide is bothersome, let me repeat the insane uttering of Hitler as he addressed his commanders on November 23, 1939 at Obersaltzburg: "After all who remembers today the extermination of the Armenians."

Before justice prevailed, six million Jews were put to death—shades of Hamid, Talaat and Enver. Hitler's "who remembers'" dastardly comment surfaced during the Nuremburg Trials after World War II, and reported in the November 24, 1945 editions of the London Times. But the Armenians, now numbering less than six million worldwide still wait for Turkey's Nuremburg Trials.

The hour was now approaching when we would be close to Erzurum. I turned to my family notes again. I wanted to be ready with the right questions, though I had been told there were no Armenians in Erzurum, my hopes still soared. Tucked in my handbook of notes, I came across comments taken from a book published in 1958 by the University of Michigan Press. Author William Yale's provocative "The Near East—A Modern History," pointed the finger of guilt at Sultan Hamid as the beast who planted the seed of genocide in the hearts and minds of the Turks.

Yale's probe at the seeding of genocide takes us back to the reign of Sultan Hamid during the time of 1894-96. During Hamid's rule the "number of Armenians—men, women, and children—slaughtered or killed as the result of exposure and starvation is variously estimated from 350,000 to 400,000 out of a total population estimated by the Armenian Church to have been 2,660,000."

Yale also writes: "There appears to be no doubt that the little group who ruled Turkey deliberately planned to rid the country of the Armenians by a policy of forced migration and wholesale slaughter. The ancient Armenian communities of Asia Minor were broken up and practically destroyed. Turkish Armenia was at an end. The Turks thought they had rid themselves forever of their Armenian Question. They did not foresee that thirty years later a prosperous Soviet Socialist Armenia would develop irredentist tendencies toward old Armenian lands in Turkey's possession."

How true, I thought. Just 12 months ago I had been to little Soviet Armenia, measuring no more than 12,500 square miles of rock, dry land and sheer human grit to survive and prosper even under the cloak of Soviet communism. Yale's description of a prosperous Armenia is accurate. If little Armenia could regain a portion of her historical lands, she could expand as a true giant of the earth. Yet these lands the Turks seized from my people remain barren. The Armenians are gone. Why have the Turks neglected this part of Anatolia? Nur remains convinced that some day the Russians will attack eastern Turkey to regain the lands for Armenia. But the truth is evident as we plowed through eastern Turkey. The Kurds now occupy most of the old Armenian settlements—and the Turkish military is seen everywhere on the pretext of fending off a Soviet attack if it ever comes. The Turkish troops are here to crush any Kurdish uprising, should the Kurds ever rise up to win statehood as had been promised by the defunct League of Nations

Just a year ago at the café of the Hotel Armenia in Yerevan I visited with present-day Hyes of Soviet Armenia, and each talked of their family roots beyond the border in Turkish-held Armenia. Like Takouhi Aslanian, a chemical engineer graduate of Yerevan State University. "My parents came from Erzurum and Kars. They were the handful who survived," the proud Armenian shared when addressing the Turkish massacres and "justice for our ancestors."

Then Sarkis Hagopian got into the discussion. "I came to Armenia in 1946 as a repatriate with my parents from Aleppo, Syria but our family roots go back to Erzurum and Kharpet, " said Hagopian, who works as a supervisor at the Hotel Armenia. He too expressed hope that "one day our people will see justice. I am proud to be here to help my country rebuild for the future."

How can I not mention Vagharshag Sarkissian, one of the most decorated artists in the Soviet Union? In our conversation last year, and hopefully when I return for another visit to Yerevan, Sarkissian bursts with pride when he speaks about earned Soviet art awards. "When I earn an honor for my paintings I let the people of the Soviet Union know that I am Armenian and damned proud of my heritage."

I was especially honored when the decorated artist invited me to his studio to sit for a painting, which has since been reproduced in a booklet of his many paintings of people and scenes in Armenia.

In my last day in Yerevan last year, Vagharshag and Takouhi took me to visit the Armenian Genocide Monument, a structure constructed on the top of a hill overlooking Yerevan. The solemn memorial consists of 12 basalt slabs that represent the 12 historic Armenian provinces in which the Turks carried out the genocide of 1915-23. I wept with my friends as we stood with bowed heads before the eternal flame.

My Soviet Armenian friends also informed me that when Turkey launched its massacres against the Armenians, the Kurdish leaders did little to help the Christian Armenians. Some actually believed their Muslim brothers, the Turks, would reward them for helping to carry out the plan of extermination. But not too long after the smoke had cleared, the Kurds sensed they would be next on Talaat's hit list, and saw that Mustafa Kemal Ataturk's founding of a Turkish Republic offered nothing to the Kurdish people. The "mountain Turks" of Turkey had cut their own wrists, and today are treated with distaste by Ankara.

Who are the Kurdish people? They're of Indo-European stock, but embrace the Muslim faith. After World War I, the western powers of Europe placed the Kurds under the jurisdiction of Turkey, Iraq and Iran. There was no free Kurdistan in their horizon, and by splitting the nomad Kurds under three separate ruling governments, hopes for a free Kurdistan was scrapped. The estimate of Kurds in southern Turkey is placed at about three million, but the Kurdish free movement leaders say they now number more than six million. . When Kurds demonstrate for freedom and human rights, they're branded as traitors in Ankara. Turkey's allies in the U.S. State Department also agree that the Kurdish movement is a terrorist campaign. I urge the Kurds to not relent in their crusade for autonomy and self-rule.

I never discussed the Kurdish problem with Mehmet. I did not want to endanger my Kurdish friend by raising the question how Turkey now mistreats his people, and labels them as "mountain Turks." I remain bewildered how Turkey can get away with the crimes she has committed against the Armenians and now the Kurdish people…thanks to their heartless clones in the U.S. State Department.

As for time capsules, there's no need to go back to 1915 to recall Turkish crimes against humanity. Let me explain. As we approached the outskirts of Erzurum, we had to pass through the town of Askele. With the world at war in 1943, Turkey was sitting it out as a so-called neutral state. Its government slapped a non-Muslim business surtax on the merchants of Istanbul. The tax was aimed at Jews, Greeks and Armenians. The business surtax was promoted to help Turkey prepare for war should it be drawn into the conflict.

When non-Muslim merchants could not pay the inflated war tax, and could not find buyers for their businesses to pay the accelerated tax, they were shipped to Askele to serve terms at hard labor. Hundreds of non-Muslim merchants were dragged off to Askele, their stores seized by the military council in Istanbul. Hundreds never returned to their families in Istanbul, until the Nazi-style labor camps were exposed by a New York Times correspondent. There's no question in my mind that the Turks got the idea for their clandestine operations by following what Hitler's street goons in the Nazi Party were carrying out at concentration camps like at Dachow. I met some of the Armenian families of Istanbul who saw loved ones taken away for failing to pay the higher taxes—and never heard from again.

At times I wanted to shout. I held my temper, but in mind and heart I cursed present-day Turkey and her allies for allowing the butchering Turk to carry on as Hamid, Enver and Talaat did. Even in 1943 against the Armenians of Istanbul while the world was at war. I know I indict all Turks when I vent my anger, but just how much can we take and not retaliate. When I returned to Detroit I asked some Istanbul Armenians about the war tax and Askele. They begged I not identify them. "We still have families there. You American Armenians are free to condemn and speak out against the Turks, but if we do, harm will come to our relatives and friends."

As we passed through Askele, my attention was now to the north, a beautiful mountain range. The color reflection gave the appearance of black, then gold. I remembered the stories my mother told me about the "black and golden mountains of Erzurum." I knew we had reached Erzurum, which the Armenians called Garin. Suddenly, for no apparent reason, Nur decided to defend Turkey. I had not uttered a word about Erzurum, and how the Turks raped the old city. But I let him speak. I wanted to hear him out. "Mr. Kehetian, the Armenians were exploited by the anti-Turkish nations of Christian Europe. Your people joined the enemy (Russia, England, France and the United States) to destroy the Ottoman Empire. I am sick and tired of being accused of killing your people. Who speaks of the thousands of Turks killed by treacherous Armenian revolutionaries who sided with the Russians. I know this is true. But the Europeans write lies about my country."

Nur's reaction was expected. He had been conditioned by his own system that Turkey had done no wrong. When I read off the list of volumes written on the massacres, Nur snapped: "I never heard of these books. If they spoke the truth my country would have put them in our schools. But lies have no place in schools." At this point I convinced Nur I had no personal hate of today's Turk. That my only question of today's

Turk is that he seek to rectify the sins of the past—as the German people are working to eradicate the bloody stain of the Nazi movement that has left Germany with scars that will mar it for several generations. Our debate subsided when we shook hands, and expressed hope that one day the Turk and Armenian can break bread at a table of resolution, but only after I urged that he ask his father what transpired in Diarbekir during the time of Hamid and Talaat. Nur's father, an educator was born and raised in Diarbekir, a city that the Armenian king, Tigranes, built in 55 B.C.

Mehmet then got into the discussion, as a peacemaker. "This is time for happiness. My dear Armenian brother, we are now in Erzurum—the birthplace of your mother. Let us rejoice. You have fulfilled the first of your oaths as a boy." He was so right. I felt exhilarated. I was in Erzurum, where my roots are very deep. Here in this eastern outpost lived the descendants of King Moushegh of Kars (962-984). According to family legend, my mother's family had traced its roots back to King Moushegh.

My maternal grandfather, Moushegh Tarpinian, was buried in Marseille, France—the victim of tuberculosis. Moushegh fled Erzurum and his native Armenia in 1905 to escape the Turks. He had been condemned to death for having aided Armenian-Russian volunteers at Kars, a rocky fortress city northeast of Erzurum. When my grandfather fled, it was the last time he would ever see his parents, brothers, sister and relatives.

With Moushegh in the flight to freedom were his wife, Surpouhi, his son Haroutune (Harry) and my mother Arousig (Alice). When the family reached Marseille, my grandfather was now battling to stay alive, not knowing his time was running out. Medical authorities told him he only has weeks, months left. My grandfather was able to purchase passage for his family to board an ocean-liner bound for America. By the time my mother got to Troy, New York where her father's friends were waiting for their arrival, word also arrived a month later that Moushegh Tarpinian had died from the dreaded disease that had attacked his body. But this "giant of the earth" lived for his family and nation. He died a hero, and ever so grateful that my baptismal name is Moushegh.

Years later, my widowed maternal grandmother married Bagdasar Mouradian. From their marriage came the birth of sons Albert and Robert. My mother loved her two "new brothers" with the care and love of a mother. To me they were Uncle Al and Uncle Bob—and I know they also treasured a brotherly bond to their "Sister Alice."

In Erzurum, my grandfather Moushegh Tarpinian was a tailor by profession. So what crime could he have committed against the ruling Turkish authority? Moushegh Tarpinian was accused of "aiding the Russian soldiers" by repairing their uniforms. He had also been branded a traitor by his activist role as a member of the Hunchak Party, an Armenian Revolutionary movement that sought freedom for the Armenians. I ask you, by what right did the Turks have to brand my grandfather a traitor. He and countless others were raising their voices for basic civil rights for the Christian Armenian population. The rights they sought were to live as free men and women in their historical homeland. The Turk arrived in Armenia at the turn of the 10th century, and by 1923 had practically erased the Armenian nation. The fucking Turks had the nerve to brand my grandfather a traitor for speaking up for his civil rights. If there are any traitors in Turkey, they're the Turkish officials and its people who still deny Ottoman Turkey waged wholesale massacres to execute the 1915 genocide of my people.

I wanted to vent my anger on Nur and Mehmet, but at this juncture in my mission it would be foolish. I remained convinced to fulfill my goal, and I still had to get to Khoops and Kutluja to authenticate the report that Parancim Keteian died several years ago, but with a faint hope that this report about her death was also incorrect as was a letter in 1922 sent to Uncle Mesrop.

We were now at the hotel. Luckily three rooms were available. Though the hotel lacked hot running water and private bath facilities, it was still a welcome sight after the ride through the towering, dangerous Manzur Mountains. Soon after we met in the hotel's coffee shop, to visit with some American tourists Nur had befriended. The Americans turned out to be Harry Crawford and Elfred Lee, in the company of several French mountain climbers. "We're headed for Mt. Ararat in search for Noah's Ark. Why not join our party. Ararat is an Armenian mountain. We should have an Armenian with our search team," Crawford suggested. Then in apparent astonishment, Crawford asked: "What in the world is an Armenian doing this far in the interior of Turkey. Aren't you afraid?"

I assured my American friends that it was perfectly safe to travel in the company of Nur and Mehmet. I declined the invitation to join their search for Noah's Ark, explaining the purpose of my mission. Crawford agreed my mission to confirm Aunt Parancim's death was a priority. I didn't come this far to go mountain climbing. But for now we chatted with Crawford's entourage, including Fernan Navarra, the celebrated French mountain climber who on a previous scaling of Mt. Ararat found carbon-tested wood which he claims came from the Biblical Noah's Ark. Nur then got into the discussion, asking Crawford whether he believed in the Ark story, and the response left my Turkish guide with a stormy expression. Crawford's answer: "Whatever lies at the bottom of the frozen glacial lake on Ararat will surely reopen the Armenian Question. If it's not the ark, then it must be some pre-glacial Armenian artifact." I knew then it was time to cut the discussion. Nur was pale, and was resenting Crawford's remarks. It was crystal clear to all at our table. In 1970 Crawford was booted out of Turkey for having been quoted in several newspapers that "Ararat belongs to the Armenians." My friendship with Crawford continued for several years until a tragic car accident in Boulder, Colorado claimed his life.

When we excused ourselves, I suggested to Nur that we find a nice restaurant to dine on some good Turkish food. After a lengthy dinner of stuffed grape leaves, shish-kebab, cracked wheat pilaf, and flat bread, we topped the night with Turkish coffee and bourma, a sweet Middle Eastern treat. Mehmet then ordered a round of drinks for a friendship toast on the night of July 22, 1969. I remembered the night with pain as I recorded my notes for the day. The pain was realizing that I was the only representative of the Armenian people in Erzurum. It was another horrifying experience . Just 64 years ago my namesake walked the cobblestone streets of Garin. Before retiring for the night I just had to challenge Nur on what happened to the Armenians. I asked: "Tell me my Turkish friend, what happened to the Armenians of Erzurum? Did they just vanish into the air, or did they die in the genocide your past Turkish leaders executed. If I am the only Armenian in Erzurum today, pray tell, what happened to them. Why can't we find any here?"

I then shared some data from my British Bluebook, and knew Nur would not find the information to his liking. But I did not care. This town was my mother's birthplace, where my grandfather lived till he was forced to flee with his family. Now I was the only Armenian. Nur knew I was tense, as I read from the Bluebook: "Out of an Armenian population estimated at 400,000 souls for the districts of Erzurum and Bitlis, not more than 10,000 survived—in other words, 98 percent of the Armenians in these districts have been deported or massacred."

Nur remained silent, with a blank expression. That night in Erzurum was the most restless night since I arrived in historical Turkish-held Armenia. I even thought of scrapping my mission, head back to Ankara, get on a plane an get the fuck out of this corrupt land of Turks who deny the past and remain silent when the Armenian issue surfaces. I felt depressed because I knew it would only get worse in the days ahead in Moush, Bitlis, Van, Keghi, and the remaining old Armenian settlements on our schedule—and in Kutluja, where the State Department airgram says Parancim Keteian lived and died just years ago. But I relented, and vowed not to let the bastard Turks scare me off. I would not quit. I had come too far. I fell asleep to music my transistor radio picked up from Yerevan, Soviet Armenia. It was clear and enriching. I also felt closer to my wife Rose, who at the same time was visiting with her Aunt Almast and cousins Noyem and Vagharshak Nikoian in Irind, a small Soviet Armenian village near the Turkish border. I soon fell asleep. In the morning, with swollen eyes, I braced myself with a vow to continue until my mission was completed. I would settle my score with the Turk by seeking justice, at whatever the cost to me. As we walked about the old eastern outpost, once described as the "Pearl of the Middle East," we came across the Erzurum Castle. My mother often spoke of the Roman castle near her father's home. There it was, the walls crumbling but the famed watchtower was still standing. This historic landmark was built in 415 A.D. on the orders of the Roman Emperor Antonius. It still stands, surviving through the centuries, earthquakes and the Turks.

Again I checked my notes to remember a strange request from an aging Armenian woman back in Michigan. Araxie Kasparian lived in the Detroit suburb of Melvindale. She knew my parents and had heard about my pending mission to Turkey. After a few phone calls, I agreed to visit Mrs. Kasparian to get information that was chilling. Erzurum was Araxie's birthplace. Her story was painful. After the massacres cleared Erzurum of its Armenians, the Turks built a train station—and stripped the area's Armenian cemeteries of all gravestones to anchor the station's floor foundation.

"When you get to Erzurum, please see if you can take pictures of the train station's floor. Look for a gravestone with my father's name. I've heard that my father's gravestone was used at the station," a tearful Mrs. Kasparian shared. I told Nur this story. He fired back: "My God, what else will you Armenians accuse my people of having committed?" At my urging Nur said he would confer with the train station mangers about Mrs. Kasparian's claim. A short time later a crestfallen Nur returned. "What the old lady told you is correct. But we can not take our cameras into the station, the military forbids it. The gravestones were used as the base of the floor and now are covered with concrete. Nothing can be seen."

Then Nur blurted a remark that startled me. I know he said it out of his own frustration, and what he had learned since we left Ankara. "Mr. Kehetian, the Armenians left years ago. What did you expect from the Turks. Were we supposed to look after the graves of the Armenians too! You Armenians were subject to Turkish rule for almost 600 years. These so-called massacres started in 1915. Tell me my Armenian brother, how come we lived peacefully for more than 500 years. As I said, the Armenians were tools of devious European powers which were out to destroy my country."

Now it was my turn. I didn't care if Nur wanted out as my guide. He was an educated young man, studying to be a lawyer. His father was an educator. I decided it was time to give it my all, and not worry about Nur's personal feeling. All I asked Nur was that he hears me out. Now I share the story with you, which is based on information I've taken from all available sources. Like I do when gathering a story or column for my newspaper—and for the information used in my manuscript, I leaned primarily on non-Armenian writers and historians. At the outbreak of World War I, Armenia was divided between Ottoman Turkey and Imperial Russia. Turkey had decided to vest its destiny with Kaiser Wilhelm's Germany. At a conference held in Ezurum the Turks called on representatives of the various Armenian national movements, with special interest in getting the Armenian Dashnak Party to support Turkey by calling on Armenians in the Russian zone to revolt. In return, after the war Armenia would be granted autonomous statehood status within the Ottoman Empire. All this was being discussed prior to Talaat's criminal orders of 1915. When the Armenian political leaders warned the Turks to stay out of the brewing war in Europe, and that it was impossible for the Dashnaks to incite a rebellion in Russian Armenia, the Turkish military was infuriated. Sensing that the Turks were determined to get into the war as Germany's ally, the Armenians pledged to do all they possibly could as loyal subjects of the Ottoman government. Unbeknown to the Armenians, their decision would be used as Talaat's excuse to remove them from the Empire by contending the Armenians would join the Russians to open a war front in Turkey's eastern districts.

Not long after the Erzurum conference, word spread throughout the Ottoman Empire that Russian-armed Armenian volunteers were advancing on the cities of Van, Bitlis, Moush and Erzurum. In Istanbul the Turks called for action. They cursed the Armenians for joining with the Russians. Talaat and his partners in crime had successfully pulled off the big lie and the enactment of the genocide plan to rid Turkey of the Armenians, and protect Turkey from an Armenian bid for statehood should the Turks lose out in the war by their partner-in-crime alliance with Germany. As for remaining loyal, the Armenians kept their word. But it still cost them with the horrific massacres that devastated historical Armenia.

Talaat's dirty tricks worked, and the Turkish people let him get away with it. That's why today's Turks deny it happened. To admit to the massacres they would be condemning their ancestors of having executed the genocide of the Armenian people. Talaat's scheme was aided by news that the Russians were advancing through the Valley of Ararat. For the Armenian in Turkey the news instilled renewed hope of ending generations of Turkish rule, and the impossible happening: freedom. The Turks were taking a beating in the war, from the Palestine front to the Balkans—and now in its eastern districts. At this point in history, Russia was still free of the Bolsheviks and their communist doctrine. Again, fate was not on Armenia's side. Lenin had seized control in Moscow, and called on Russian troops in Eastern Europe and on the Turkish front to "return to Mother Russia." For the Armenians, panic set in. As the Russians withdrew, the Turks advanced and slaughtered all who stood in their way.

President Wilson had dubbed the Armenians as "our Little Ally," though the United States and Turkey had not declared a state of war between the two nations. Just when it appeared the end had finally erased the Armenian race, now the fate of justice was swinging in Armenia's favor. Kaiser Germany agreed to an armistice with the Allied Powers, and had given up on its dream of building a train line from Berlin to Baghdad—which would have plowed through the very heart of historical Armenia.

But the Turks still sought to erase the Armenian Question, and set out to destroy the remaining Armenian foothold in the Caucasus. Deserted by the Russians, the Armenians rallied for their very salvation. In three major battles with the advancing Turkish army, the Armenians decided to concentrate their last stand at the village of Sardarabad. If the Turks win, then they will enter Etchmiadzin, site of the Holy See of the Armenian Church, and advance to the very gates of Yerevan. For six days the Armenians held their position. On the seventh day the Turks were turned back and in retreat. Armenia was saved. For Armenians the independence of May 28, 1918 has been enshrined for all time. A crippled Armenian military, facing a superior Turkish troop force, fought its greatest battle for freedom. After nearly two million slaughtered, its historical lands left barren and depopulated the Armenian finally won his independence to end Turkish oppression that started at the turn of the 10th century.

During the war and massacres, Erzurum suffered greatly. The city changed hands six times during the Turkish-Russian conflict. The last time Erzurum was free of the Turks was in August of 1916. When the legendary Armenian military commander General Antranik entered Erzurum after two weeks of fighting, he found only 100 Armenians still alive. The streets and rivers were filled with Armenian corpses. They were the victims of the retreating Turks. Men who served with the Armenian general tell this story: "When Antranik found the thousands of slain Armenians, he fell to his knees and wept. As he wept before his troops, he vowed to God to avenge his people at whatever the cost." There aren't too many Armenians left who can trace their ancestry to Erzurum. The entire populace was removed, killed and violated of all basic human rights.

To perpetuate the legacy of Erzurum, a handful of survivors of old Garin published a history of their birthplace. They want future generations to know that Erzurum was an Armenian city, and was described as the "Pearl of the Middle East." Yet when I walked the streets of Erzurum, I remember reading how Victor Hugo defined it: " The Turk has trodden this land, all is in ruins..."

We were now on the road, headed for Van. I asked Mehmet to stop the car. I wanted to fill an empty film container with the soil of Erzurum to place on mother's grave at the Woodmere Cemetery in Detroit. Without a word, Nur took the container from my hand, and said: "Give me the honor of gathering the soil to express my prayers to your dear mother."

I closed my eyes, and cried for Erzurum. The Turk must pay for what his ancestors did to my people. By denial, today's Turk remains equally guilty of Talaat's crimes—and to my last breath I will seek justice. Hopefully this memoir will arouse the hearts and minds of human rights activists in present-day Turkey.

CHAPTER EIGHT

The drive to the low-lands of fertile Moush and Lake Van was a solemn journey. Nur and Mehmet tried to cheer me up with words of praise for having embarked on a mission to visit the birthplaces of my mother and father, and especially to be certain Parancim, my father's sister, had died as reported in the State Department airgram. My two friends also shared hope that my father's sister might still be alive, and reassured me that in a few more days we will be in Keghi province to confirm the airgram report. But my thoughts were still focused on Erzurum, rapidly vanishing in sight as we headed in a southerly direction. We were now five miles out of Erzurum when I offered a silent prayer to its massacred people, and that in some future generation of my family tree another descendant of Moushegh Tarpinian will walk the same paths I had taken in my bonding with the home of my namesake—and my mother's birthplace. But when that future of hope comes to life, Erzurum will be free again and reattached to present-day Armenia as President Woodrow Wilson had drafted for the League of Nations.

An hour had now passed when Mehmet announced we were about to cross the Arax River, and come upon the small Kurdish village of Henis. We decided to stop at a mountain spring for some fresh water. No sooner said, our car was quickly surrounded by the children from the village. They smiled and clapped hands. When Nur told the children I was an Armenian from America, they then came forth to clasp hands with me. By this time some elders from the village also came over to check out the commotion. One old man said the Armenians used to talk about a legend that the spring we had just fetched water to quench our thirst was "a holy spring." They said an Armenian saint, St. Gregory the

Illuminator, had spoken to God by the very same mountain spring and drank its water. I asked Nur to question them on how they knew about the Armenian saint, the response was penetrating: "The Armenians who used to live here told our fathers about their saint talking to God." Nur then asked who was St. Gregory the Illuminator and what happened "to those Armenians." The friendly Kurdish villager replied softly: "They died in the war…"

I answered Nur's question about St. Gregory. The Armenian saint founded the Christian faith in Armenia 301 A. D. He then served as its very first "Catholicos of All Armenians" at the Holy See in Etchmiadzin. The village children had me surrounded, and like kids anywhere, they were excited and full of laughter. I took several packs of chewing gum from my travel case, and quickly handed one stick to each child. These were good kids. Each one bowed as I handed them the gum. They were happy even with one stick. And they whispered: "Ermanie, Ermanie, Ermanie.." Nur told me Ermanie is the Turkish and Kurdish name for Armenians. He then stressed that "these little children have heard the story of the Armenian saint who talked to God at this spring. Now they have met an Armenian for the first time. They'll remember this day for many years."

Just before we left Henis, I splashed some of the cool spring water on my face. Mehmet said "now the water of your Armenian saint is upon you. You will be blessed forever, and God will protect you from harm." My Kurdish friend then said we were getting close to Lake Van. You will love the blue water of Lake Van. Like your Armenian blue eyes, the waters of Van are sparkling blue."

After several hours on the winding road to the town of Tatvan, resting along the western shoreline of Lake Van, my eyes focused on the lake Armenians worshipped. Words can not frame for you the beauty of this large body of salt water. It was stunning. Once at the shoreline, I rinsed my hands in the salty waters of Van—and offered a prayer for the men and women of Van who stood tall for days in resisting the Turkish bloodbath of 1915. We then decided to press our luck to go further, though the roads were crowded with Turkish military trucks. If successful at reaching the eastern side of lake, Mehmet said we would be able to see the Island of Aghtamar, spirited by a legend of love that ranks at the top in romantic Armenian folklore. Then we would drive to the heartland of the Armenian nation, the heroic city of Van—and birthplace of the ancient Urartu civilization. But our hopes were dashed a short distance down the road past Tatvan. The road to Van was closed. Turkish "war games" were being waged. You could hear the shelling in the distant mountains. Then we saw a convoy of armored trucks, and American-made half-tracks driven by Turkish soldiers.

The story of Van is deeply etched into the history of ancient Urartu, authored by Russian scholar Boris Piotrovsky in 1969. The masterful effort was accurately titled about the "Ancient Civilization of Urartu." To know about the heroic Armenians of Van, students of history must read the scholarly work of the Russian author.

The detour to Van even saddened Nur. "I really wanted to see the city of Van. My father told me Van's history goes back into Biblical time. The people of ancient Urartu once lived in Van. Did the Armenians ever live in Van?" I bite my tongue. If Hrayr Toukhanian was with me he could give Nur a lesson in the history of Van and its heroic people. Hrayr traces his family roots to Van, and is an active member of the national society in Detroit that perpetuates the legacy of Van—and knows the history of Van from its glory days to its destruction in 1915 by the Turks. My friend Hrayr, a film producer in Detroit, has interviewed Armenian survivors of Van in Beirut where he was born and at national meetings of the society in the United States and Canada. I regretted not being able to get to Van to take some pictures for Hrayr, and his fellow Vanetzee comrades.

At Nur's urging that I tell him about the people of Van, I again turned to my British Bluebook to report that in 1915 the Armenians were the majority in numbers with nearly 30,000. The Turkish-Kurdish population was pegged at 20,000. When the Turks recaptured the burning city on the night of August 4, 1915 less than 1,000 Armenians still lived. The Bluebook also tells us that about 5,000 fortunate citizens of Van were able to escape the Turkish onslaught by fleeing with the retreating Russian troops into the Caucasus Mountains—in what today is Soviet Armenia.

The heroic citizens of Van were the first to raise their fists against the Turks. Not in a revolt, but to defend their people. The Turkish governor of Van was a fiend named Djevdet Bey. This is what the Bluebook says about the defense and death of Van: "The evidence makes it clear that there was no unprovoked insurrection of the Armenians at Van, as the Ottoman Government asserts in its official apologia. The Armenians only took up arms in self-defense, and the entire responsibility for the outbreak rests with Djevdet Bey, the local governor—whether he was acting on his own initiative or was simply carrying out instructions from Constantinople." The Bluebook also makes mention that Bey was a brother-in-law of Enver Pasha, thus cementing the belief that the orders to exterminate Van of all Armenians came right from the top—the Ottoman Turkish government.

At Detroit Vanetzee functions when folk dance music was being played, we could always count on Yervant Kazarian, a genocide survivor, to lead the dance to show the steps required to dance to the village music and perform the "Vanetzee bar as it should be danced." Here on the western shoreline of Lake Van, the vision was clear to me. I imagined Mr. Kazarian was leading the Vanetzee dance but without smiles as he did so often at a church function back home. Instead I saw tears. The tears were for his massacred brothers and sisters of Van.

Nur was silent. No questions. No emotion. No rebuttal. Instead he merely shrugged: "We should be in Moush in another 20 minutes or so. We will stay there tonight. We will find the villages of your wife's parents. According to my map, there is a nice hotel in Moush. It is run by the Ministry of Tourism, and hopefully we can bathe with hot water tonight."

By his tone of voice I knew the report on Van did not go well with Nur. I did not press the issue. But what irked Nur the most was telling him how the Vanetzee spirit lives wherever descendants of Van live—from Beirut to Fresno to Detroit. And that they hold annual conferences, grant scholarships to college-bound students and when the band plays the dance music of Van, the floor is jammed with young people to dance to the music their ancestors did in Van.

We hadn't gone but five miles when Mehmet stopped, turned to me asking "would you like to see Bitlis. I can make it in an hour. Then we can go to Moush. Since we can not get to Van, Bitlis will make up for it. It's a beautiful city. They also have some of the finer restaurants in Anatolia. I promise you will enjoy it, even for a few hours." I agreed, and immediately thought of Vrej Nersessian at the St. Sarkis Church in London. His wish will come true. Now I can fulfill the promise I made to the young Etchmiadzin seminarian graduate. I would visit the birthplace of his family's roots, and take some pictures. Nersessian impressed me as an artistically talented member of the church who would serve with excellence in the British culture. More importantly, he too shared the common link that bonds all Armenians. We are all linked to the genocide. The pattern of genocide in Turkish-held Armenia was repeated in Bitlis too, as documented in the Bluebook: "There was no pretense here of deportation, and the Armenians were destroyed, without regard for appearances, by outright massacre, accompanied in many cases of torture."

When the Russians withdrew along the entire eastern Turkish front, Bitlis was included for a deathly blow. When the Turks reentered the city on June 25, 1915 the bloodbath began. The British Bluebook then tells us that with "the stroke of the Turkish sword, more than 15,000 Armenians perished. The same fate fell upon the adjoining Armenian villages of Rahva and Khoultig."

At a quaint Kurdish restaurant we were served the finest meal of our journey. Stuffed grape leaves and tomatoes—smothered with madzoon (yogurt) and piping hot rice pilaf filled our plates. Many of the table foods of the Kurds, Turks and Armenians are similar in taste and preparation. Living in the same region for several centuries had a lot to do with it. But it ended there, triggered by what was about to happen in 1915.

The history of Bitlis dates back to the Urartu Era, the early forming years of the Armenian race. Some of the officials in Bitlis told Nur that at least 5,000 Armenians live in the outlying villages, but that few, if any live in Bitlis. Tragically those Armenians can not speak in their native tongue. It is forbidden to teach any language other than Turkish, and a good number of the Armenian survivors are women who were taken as wives of the Kurds and Turks and raised to embrace the Muslim faith. Where the genocide failed, the ethnic cleansing succeeded. On entering Bitlis you must cross under a towering mountain citadel crumbing with age and neglect. The awe-inspiring citadel was built by the Urartuans, rebuilt by Alexander the Great, and finally destroyed by the first waves of the Seljuks. Because of its strategic location, the citadel was named the Bitlis Pass.

As I photographed some of the picturesque sights of Bitlis, including the swift running brook that sliced right through the heart of the town, I spotted a black horse at the highest point of the citadel. I pointed it out to Nur and asked why the Turks let the horse roam loose when such animals were considered a prize. Nur already knew the answer: "The people of Bitlis consider the mountaintop citadel a place of evil spirits. I was told the black horse never leaves the citadel's plateau and the natives say the horse has been taken over by the evil spirits." But Nur, I prodded, what kind of evil spirits would scare the brave Turks?" Again, Nur responded: "One of the merchants told me the spirits of the dead Armenians haunt the old fortress, and now control the horse." I couldn't let that one slip away without commenting: "Nur, I thought only the Kurdish mountain Turks were superstitious." He just grinned.

Now it was time to head for Moush, which the Turks renamed to Mus. As Nur had promised the hotel in Moush was modern but again, no hot water. But by now I was getting used to cold baths. We had no choice. We arrived in Moush after sundown, and decided just to grab a sandwich after we took baths. In the morning we would search for the villages of Sogkom and Marnik, the birthplaces of Rose's parents and walk through what is left of the Armenian section of Moush. In Armenian history the people of Moush are praised for their devout faith in the church. The defenders of Moush are admired for having taken heroic stands against the murdering Turks. Descendants of Moush also take great pride in reminding fellow Armenians that it took the wisdom of one of their own, St. Mesrop, to create an alphabet for the Armenians.

The Bluebook tells that the massacres of Moush began June 28, 1915. No one was spared, "not even the orphans in the German Orphanage . Even the Rev. Krikor and Marcar Ghougasian, teachers at the orphanage were killed. The Turks then opened the tomb of Sourp. Garabed and destroyed everything. Rather than heed an appeal that he escape to avoid certain death with several monks, the father superior of Sourp Garabed, Yeghishe Vartabed, was killed with the local population. He died with his flock.

After a hearty breakfast, we went searching for Armenians in central Moush's marketplace. We found a little, balding old man who answered to the name of Hagop. The date was July 23, 1969. Hagop's life story was another footnote in the Armenian genocide: "My son, the most Armenians we still have here is about 15. We are all old and have taken the Muslim faith. We had no choice. What else could we do. This was once a great Armenian city. I still remember my classmates. But I survived because a Kurdish family protected me. The Kurds say the Armenians were a majority before the war, but when we die then Moush will die."

Hagop then offered to show me a few Armenian landmarks that still stand, though most were crumbling—like the Sourp Garabed Church still standing with its walls and roof. We even found the church seminary of Moush, the Armenian inscription above the entrance, though whitewashed, was still visible. It now serves as a warehouse for farmers. In less than 30 minutes I saw the stark naked result of genocide. Nothing left to tell a passing traveler that once a nation of Armenians lived on these lands and that Moush was one of the major centers of Armenian life—dating back to pre-Biblical time. That from Moush the Armenian alphabet was given life by its creator, St. Mashtotz.

The gory details of the massacres that swept across the plains of Moush can be found in countless volumes, scholarly and researched— from the priceless work of Arnold J. Toynbee's "Armenian Atrocities—The Murder of a Nation," to this effort by an American born Armenian who is not a scholar, who just happens to be the son of survivors of the Armenian genocide and believes that the hand of fate motivated my mission to bring me to the ancestral homeland. I walked the same paths and trails my people were dragged through the time span of 1915-23. Even now I feel the pain I endured during the time I walked through Moush. The celebrated writer-historian Toynbee describes many scenes of despair, in particular the day the Murad River spilled over its banks because the shallow river had been the dumping site for thousands of corpses, leading to the flooding of the low plains of Moush.

Again I turned to my British Bluebook to share with Nur and Mehmet the suffering inflicted upon the people of Moush: "The massacres of Moush were directed by Governor Djevdet Bey of Van, Commander Halil of Diliman, Governor Abdul Khalak of Bitlis, and Governor Servet Bey of Moush. The order for massacre was given on June 28, 1915. According to Turkish government statistics 120,000 Armenians were killed in this district." Nur just sat silent. I then shared my notes from Toynbee's "Murder of a Nation," which was equally chilling to the bone: "Of the Armenian people as a whole we may put an estimate that three-fourths are gone, and these three-fourths includes the leaders in every walk of life. The extermination of the race seems to be the objective, and the means employed are more fiendish than could be concocted locally. The orders are from headquarters, and any reprieve must be from the same source..."

But as we continue this journey, I hope to share with you the hope and faith of my people. I believe the message of the great writer-humanitarian, Anatole France, delivered at a gathering of distinguished French leaders and intellectuals at the Sorbonne in Paris, expresses the feeling of Armenians worldwide. Though said in 1916, the message remains bold and was worded to carry on until justice is achieved. While describing Armenia's plight, Anatole France said "Armenia is in agony. But it will rise again. The little blood remaining in it is invaluable, future generations of valorous heroes will be born from it."

I have a special attachment and feeling for the Armenians of Moush. My wife Rose traces her family tree to the Moush villages of Sogkom and Marnik. She is a dedicated soldier for the Armenian cause, and from the time we first met, Rose shared her Moush pride by reiterating if God blessed us with children they would be raised to embrace their

Armenian heritage—as she was raised by her genocide surviving parents. As Hagop walked us through the Armenian section of Moush that still stands, I knew Rose was visiting with her relatives in Soviet Armenia. I took as many pictures that time allowed. Now it was time to find the villages of Sogkom and Marnik. Nur was able to get the information we needed to find Sogkom, which was less than a mile from central Moush. Here in this farming village lived Mesrop Sarkisian—the son of Sarkis and Siranoush Maligian. Long before his death in the western Pennsylvania steel-producing town of Ambridge, situated on the banks of the Ohio River just north of Pittsburgh, Mesrop Sarkisian told me the stories of his beloved village of Sogkom.

After our marriage in Ambridge, I was able to convince Rose's father to share with me what happened in Sogkom when the Turks pillaged the village. I'm glad I took notes. I did that in my job as a newspaper reporter. The life story Mesrop Sarkisian shared with me was sacred and needed to be saved and told to his grandchildren. It was a cruel life. Somehow he had survived to start a new life in America. He built his own home, brick by brick, to provide the best possible home for his wife and daughters Ann, Rose and Irene. Mesrop died before I journeyed to his birthplace in Moush province. I am ever so thankful to have had the wisdom to keep my notes, which I now share with you. An attachment of Turkish irregulars had come to his father's village. The Turks wanted to increase the tax levy. Here is the story, as told by my wife's father: "When my father told the Turks our crops were poor in the previous year, that he did not have enough to earn a profit at the markets in Moush they cursed the entire village. Then when my father told them he could not pay the higher tax, the Turks opened fire on our home. Soon the entire village erupted into bloodshed. The Turks used their guns and bayonets to kill the villagers. I saw them kill my parents, my four older brothers. Some of the village children were able to escape to the mountains. I could not move. One of the Turks drove a bayonet into me just above my right hip. The blood was oozing out. I could not stop the bleeding. I fell to the ground just outside our farm house. I knew my time had come. All I could hear was people crying—and dying while the Turks were ransacking our homes."

But Mesrop Sarkisian lived to tell the story of death to his family and the village of Sogkom. A Kurdish farmer from an adjoining field who tilled the soil with his father found Mesrop near the Maligian farmhouse. At first he thought his friend's son was dead, but saw Mesrop was still breathing while unconscious. The Turks left with whatever they could steal from the pillaged village, and vanished like a pack of killer bees. Somehow the friendly Kurd was able to get Mesrop to his own home, and successful at getting the bleeding to stop. Mesrop was saved. But for the remaining days in his life, he walked with a limp from the bayonet wound. After recovering from his wound, Mesrop escaped across the Turkish line into then Mesopotamia, now Iraq. With the help of Armenians Mesrop finally made his way to Aleppo and from there to set out for his new life in America. Friendly Syrian doctors treated Mesrop to help prepare him for the long journey to America. Mesrop was able to elude Turkish police in Aleppo before boarding a French vessel bound for a new life in America…Even now I can see Mesrop Sarkisian limping up the church aisle to present his daughter's hand to me in marriage. I will treasure that day till my last. He had survived hell on earth, but that day at the Holy Trinity Greek Orthodox Church in Ambridge, Pa. Mesrop was smiling.

The village of Sogkom is now occupied by Kurdish mountain people who were ordered by the Turks in 1939 to leave their mountain outpost and settle in the vacant Armenian village. They were told to grow onion crops, which the village was famous for when the Armenians farmed the rich land and hence the crowning of Sogkom's name after onions. As we walked through the village it was a sickening site to behold. The same mud and straw huts from the turn of the century, and a stench fueled by the intense July sun penetrating mounds of cow manure being stored for heating fuel in the winter season. Even Nur was shocked at the conditions we were encountering and said it loudly: "In the name of Allah,. There is filth everywhere."

Soon the village elders were upon us, questioning our presence. After explaining why we had come to Sogkom, the Kurdish leader of the village invited us into his home. It was the largest one we could see, with the quarters for his livestock in the adjoining stretch of the mud and stone dwelling. Soon we exchanged chocolates for Turkish coffee and sweet pastries, as Nur told the friendly Kurdish chieftain about me and my mission to find Sogkom. The tall, muscular Kurd then reached out to my hand to express a Kurdish handshake of friendship. Then with Nur interpreting, the village chieftain told us this harrowing story: "When the government told my people to settle in this village, they said it once had an Armenian chieftain named Sarkis Maligian. As a matter of fact, you are in the home of that man named Sarkis Maligian."

I clenched my fists, as a hundred thoughts of violence flashed through my mind. If I had been armed, I would have silenced everyone in that house that was once the home of my father-in-law's family. Nur placed his hand on my shoulder. I could see the chilling information he had just interpreted was equally offensive to him, and he pleaded I remain silent so he could get more information. Nur then told the Kurdish chieftain that Sarkis Maligian was my wife's grandfather. In responding, the Kurd, in a note of sincerity, said: "You must come back with your family. This home belongs to your wife. Her grandfather must have been a strong and wise man to be the chieftain of this village, which was famous for its onion crop." By now my temper had cooled. How could I blame the Kurds for what the Turks carried out in the massacres, yet I also knew from every available textbook that overall the Kurdish population also cashed in on the plight of my people. They stole what valuables the Armenians had even while being driven on foot in death marches, took their vacated homes and farms and even assisted in the killing of innocent people—a crime against humanity that was repeated just 30 years later while prison guards at Nazi Germany's concentration camps said they had nothing to do with Hitler's executioners who murdered six million European Jews. How pathetic, now the Kurds are suffering and ridiculed as mere "mountain Turks."

Once outside the "home of Sarkis Maligian," the tears were swelling from my eyes. Again the horror of the past was in my mind, and this chapter even closer to our family. I fumbled for a cigarette, but one of the Kurdish chieftain's sons stepped up, offering me a Turkish-blend cigarette. He knew I was shaken by what his father told me. As my eyes focused on the mountains of Moush, still glittering with snow on some of their highest levels, I cringed. I wanted to shout to a silent God who did not answer the prayers of Sogkom and all of Armenia. I cried that while my people were being slaughtered, the first nation to have embraced Christianity as its state religion, no one came to its aid. All that was said were mere words of compassion, and broken promises. Nur now sensed it was time to leave: "I think you've seen enough of this village my Armenian brother. Let's go find Marnik and Norsha."

Before we left Sogkom, I filled another empty film container with the soil of this village that eventually found its way to the grave of Mesrop Sarkisian at a cemetery in Ambridge. As we walked toward Mehmet's car, the Kurdish chieftain again clasped my hands and offered a prayer for a safe return to my home in America. Now he knew the true story of Sarkis Maligian, and that the village had been terrorized by Turkish irregulars in 1915 with violence and killings—and how a friendly Kurd helped save one of Sarkis Maligian's wounded sons, who years later, walking with a limp, gave his daughter in marriage. Yes, the survivors of the Armenian genocide are truly the giants of the earth.

Now we were headed to Marnik, where Rose's mother was born. It was here that an Armenian girl, Hripsimeh Bedrosian, was raised and forced to flee during the massacres with her younger sister Almast. Hripsimeh and Almast were orphaned by the Turkish sword—and separated for the remaining days of their lives. Hripsimeh, my wife's mother, along with a handful of other orphaned children from Moush were gathered by Christian missionaries and taken to Greece, while her sister, Almast, was picked up by Armenians headed for Yerevan, then under the control and protection of Russia. The two sisters did not learn of each other having survived until the 1950's when Armenian repatriates reported that Almast Bedrosian was alive and living in the Soviet Armenian village of Irind.

Like her husband's vision of the homeland, Hripsimeh remained blurred by the bloody past. When she recalled the day blood spilled in Marnik, Rose's mother remembered when the Turks came upon her village. People screamed for mercy, children prayed for God to save them, but the killing continued. The last time she saw her father, Mourad Bedrosian, he was being led away by the Turks, and never seen again. She never knew what happened to her mother Manooshag. When Rose found her Aunt Almast in 1968, she was also at a loss at not knowing what happened to the Bedrosian family. Most of the village people in Irind traced their roots to the Moush region, refugees and orphans. As for Marnik, the response was the same: "No Ermanie…" Again I filled an empty film container with the soil of Marnik for Hripsimeh's grave.

I still had one more village to find if time permitted. We wanted to leave for Bingol by sunset to avoid having to drive into the late hours of the night. Mehmet was also concerned about the poor road conditions, making them dangerous at night. But we were fortunate to find Norsha on our way back to central Moush. In the town of Ambridge, my wife's parents were especially fond of a fellow Armenian, Samuel Arakelian. Samuel was born and raised in Norsha village and like thousands of other refugee Armenians had found his way to America and western Pennsylvania. I knew Samuel would be thrilled to know I found his village and returned with pictures and soil. I found more than a village. We found one Armenian still living. Like a miracle, the man was a boyhood friend of Samuel. This lone Armenian of Norsha, Boghos Segoian, welcomed me with open arms. Quickly he sent for refreshments, and repeated and repeated: "By the grace of God I have been honored with the visit of an Armenian." In our visit, resting in the shade of an oasis he had built on his farm, Boghos said he remembered Samuel Arakelian. He then motioned to the left of his farm, "that land over there belonged to Samuel's father. As boys we worked the fields of our fathers and became friends. I always thought Samuel died during the war. Our families were friends and we went to the same church in Moush, it was the Sourp Garabed Church. But the Turks burned it during the war. I still recite the prayers I learned as a boy. That's how I kept my sanity when the Turks killed my family. That's how I have been able to retain my Armenian language, through the prayers of my church. But when I die, that will be the end. My sons have been raised as Muslims by their Kurdish mother. There was no other choice. When I die I will join my family and people who were killed by the

Turks. And the only reason I survived to live was because of friendly Kurds."

How does one respond to that kind of despair. All I could do to bolster this old man's spirit was to share that the Armenians in Soviet Armenia live in peace and that life promises them a better future, even under communism. Boghos' eyes twinkled with joy when I told him that the Armenians of America work steadily to retain their identity through churches, schools and community centers that serve the Armenian community. But in a tone of sorrow, Boghos whispered, softly: "When I die Armenia dies in this village. My wife is a Kurd, my sons think like Kurds. The fate that crushed my family and our people now waits to strike me in my old age. Sometimes I've cried myself to sleep, asking Astvadz (God) why he didn't let me die with my family." The hour to depart for Bingol was now upon us, Boghos quickly instructed his sons to get some soil to send back to his Armenian friend in America. "Take this soil to Samuel, and tell him nothing is left of the Norsha we knew as children. Please tell my boyhood friend I remember him, and will until I close my eyes." As we embraced the two of us wept. Just how much more can I take before I get out of Turkish-held Armenia. Village after village the story repeats itself, while the fucking Turks in Ankara gloat that they had nothing to do with the massacres and genocide of 1915.

After a short distance down the road, we crossed the Mourad River and the writing of Toynbee flashed again: "…the river went over its banks because the corpses of Armenians had jammed the bend in the river…" Yet that day we crossed the river, it was serene.

A year later in revisiting Soviet Armenia I searched for survivors of Moush. One such survivor was Antranig Parseghian, a retired painter living in Yerevan. Parseghian told me "when the Turks and Germans opened artillery fire on Moush, the sky turned red from the spiraling flames. My father died fighting against the Turks. Only the courage of my mother saved us. When we reached Yerevan, disease and hunger was rampant. But we survived. In reliving the family's escape to freedom, Parseghian tells a story often recited by survivors of Moush. At the height of the Turkish attack on Moush, the German artillery commanders suggested to their Turkish ally : "Give us two hours and those Armenians will surrender. The shells from our guns will level all in sight." The Germans were right. When the Armenians sent word they had fought their last fight, the Turks insisted that the German artillery gunners continue to bombard the Armenian section. It was then that an unknown German officer uttered the words that they should "save a few Armenians for the museums." The Turks weren't amused. They were infuriated. They demanded the guns to continue firing." Then Parseghian smiled. "In the final blow at defeating the Nazi's in World War II came when Russian tanks entered Berlin. One of the tanks was driven by an Armenian from Yerevan. His ancestors were from Moush. After blasting away the last barrier to Hitler's bunker, the Armenian tank commander inscribed on the battered wall of a building a message that read: "The Armenians survived the museums…"

Antranig Parseghian's brother was the father of famed Notre Dame football coach, Ara Parseghian. My friendship with Antranig was heightened when we discovered that one of his cousins in Yerevan had married one of my wife's cousins. By Armenian protocol, that made us cousins. Several years later when the famed Notre Dame Football coach was in Detroit to address a sporting event, I approached him on stage before the program to pass on some pictures of his cousins in Yerevan. Ara Parseghian beamed: "Hey, we even look alike."

The legendary Notre Dame Football coach then shared the pictures with fellow sports panel members. For Parseghian the pictures quickly called for a time out to give the coach of the Fighting Irish time to brag about his "cousins in Armenia."

As for the city of Moush, it lives no more. Just in the hearts of the people who still trace their family roots to the historic Armenian community. One such example was the pastor of my church back in Detroit, Rev. Souren Papakhian . This dear servant of the church, now in Heaven, loved Moush. When Rev. Papakhian died, Armenian church leaders from throughout the United States and Canada came to the St. Sarkis Church to bid their church brother a deserving farewell. For three days the church was crowded with young and old alike to mourn his death and celebrate his life. The Armenian church leader was noted for sermons with a tone of nationalism in leading the cause for justice. Frequently he reminded the congregation that "the Armenian Church is a national church. It must lead the fight for justice." Before his last days, Rev. Papakhian visited Soviet Armenia. On his return the son of Moush told me "our people have found new hope. Armenia still lives. Our people survived the genocide. We will survive from communism."

I ask again, how we can forget. We can not forget because justice remains to be served. The souls of nearly two million Armenians serve as a living memory. I may never see Moush again, but this dear old city burns in my heart. It burns in the hearts of all Armenians, for it was in Moush a scholarly church leader invented the Armenian alphabet. It is said the faith of the Armenian, their unique alphabet and will to survive has kept them out of history's archives as a mere footnote of the past.

To those who say Armenians need to get off the genocide hype with Turkey, I can only repeat we can not forget. We can not until the Turk seeks to correct Turkey's past crimes against humanity. By hiding in a state of denial, the crime will not vanish. Only justice will erase the crime and spur the healing process for closure. I repeat my position to members of the U.S. Congress who say we should not offend the Turk with a crime that happened in 1915.

Getting Turkey to acknowledge the genocide will only open the door to full recovery and justice. The lands of Wilson Armenia and the May 28, 1918 Armenian Republic must be resolved. Those lands were seized with no resistance because Talaat's plan of genocide had left historical Armenia a land barren of its people. We need more than words of forgiveness and compassion. That's why the Turk refuses to admit to the truth, by doing she must then negotiate the return of portions of the lands seized by carrying out the genocide.

The purpose of the genocide was sinister, dehumanizing. But for the Turk it worked at achieving its goal.

Now Turkey must pay for her sins of the past.

She must be held accountable and punished for the crime of genocide as mandated by the Genocide Convention rule adopted in 1948 by the General Assembly of the United Nations. Punishment for committing the crime of genocide has no time limit of expiration. As a member of the UN's General Assembly, Turkey should know the meaning of international law. That's why present-day Turkey remains stuck in its state of denial.

CHAPTER NINE

The long-awaited journey to Bingol, known as the city of a thousand lakes, was now in motion. Mehmet's sturdy Chevy had no trouble in driving through the low-lands between Moush and Bingol, but once in Bingol we knew the mountains extending from the city in a northwardly direction to Kutluja would be hazardous and challenging. Though in actual mileage we were no more than 80 miles away from our destination, Mehmet said the drive would take at least two hours because of the intense July heat could place a drain on the car's radiator system. I told Mehmet to drive with caution. This was no time to force the car engine to overheat driving up the winding mountains that were ahead. But confident Mehmet said we should not worry. "Tonight we will be in Bingol. After a good night's rest, we drive up the mountains to Keghi to find your cousins and your father's birthplace in Khoops." Mehmet and Nur shared my excitement. The three of us, a Kurd, a Turk and an Armenian bonded like brothers. We were now about to find out if Parancim still lives, or died several years ago as the consulate airgram had reported.

But before we continue on this journey, let me stress that in the same year I ventured out into the interior of historical Armenia, renown writer Howard M. Sachar had just completed his thought-provoking book of academic knowledge entitled 'The Emergence of the Middle East— 1914-1924." A book in which he devoted several chapters to "The Armenian Genocide" and the causes that led to the extermination attempt.

The Harvard-educated teacher-writer also penned moving volumes on the people of Israel. As we proceed on to Bingol and

Kutluja, the purpose of my being in Turkey in the summer of 1969, I would like to share with you some of Sachar's descriptions of the massacres.

First, let's discuss the actual number of victims of that first genocide of the 20th century. While the actual count has no bearing, and the Armenian does not relish playing the numbers game over his massacred people—the numbers question frequently arises. You can find texts that list the total figure from one to two million. Sachar, using data made available to him by his scholarly study, says "Of the most thoroughly documented surveys, Dr. Johannes Lepsius calculated the total of Armenians slain or deported as 1,396,000."

Dr. Lepsius, at the height of the massacres, served as chief of the Protestant Mission in the Ottoman Empire. Like the then American Ambassador Henry Morgenthau, this compassionate mission leader pleaded to Talaat that he cease in his plan of extermination. But like Morgenthau's plea, his appeal was also was s shunned by a hateful man embarked on a sinister plot against the human race.

Even in writing about the retaliatory measures the Armenians took against the Turks of Erzurum, Sachar defined the Armenian action against the Turks as "the last and only revenge the Armenians would ever achieve for their crucifixion." How then does Sachar describe the death of Turkish-held Armenia. He states: "British scholar and foreign office expert Arnold Toynbee places the number of those killed as more accurately between 800,000 and 1,000,000. In either case, not more than a third of the Armenian population of 1914 remained in Turkey when the war ended. By any standards this was surely the most unprecedented, indeed the most unimaginable racial annihilation, until then, in modern history."

Continuing, Sachar writes: "Nevertheless, apparently unconcerned by the enormity of their affront to civilization, members of the Young Turk regime continued to view the deportations as nothing more than effective diplomacy, the realization of Abdul Hamid's injunction that "the best way to finish the Armenian Question is to finish with the Armenians."

While condemning the Young Turk movement as a carry-over of Hamid's insidious policies, Sachar also points a finger of guilt in the direction of Germany. Let me repeat this critical segment: "What was astonishing, rather, was the efficiency and speed with which the notoriously inept Turkish bureaucracy engineered a liquidation of these dimensions. Moreover, it is of interest that the genocide was cited approvingly twenty-five years later by the Fuhrer of the identical European nation who found the Armenian 'solution' an instructive precedent for a campaign of even broader scope and finality against another people."

Sachar also documents that August day back in 1914 at Erzurum when Turkish representatives conferred with officials of the Armenian Dashnak Party—in hopes of luring the Armenians into the war. While the Dashnaks pledged to support the Empire's war ambitions, they rejected the plan to incite Russian Armenians to revolt against the tsarist rule in the Caucasus. Meanwhile the other two major Armenian political movements kept a close watch of the outcome of the conference to determine if the Turks had other motives. The Hunchak and Ramgavar parties were on target, and quickly alerted their followers to be on guard for violence. The Dashnaks were also suspicions that the Ottoman government was plotting to renew Hamid's solution to the Armenian Question.

In looking at that decision made by the Dashnak leaders, Sachar concludes: "The Turkish emissaries thereupon left Erzurum and returned to Constantinople empty-handed. Learning of the Dashnak response, the Turkish leaders made little effort to disguise their chagrin and outrage. Their reaction, in turn, immediately had its impact on the anxious and distraught Armenian population. Leaders of the three Armenian political parties were now defenseless. The Russians had retreated from the Turkish front, but the Turks were being dealt heavy blows on the Persian and Palestine fronts by British forces supported with Assyrian and Armenian volunteers."

Meanwhile the growing fear of the three Armenian political parties was about to strike the people. The impact was put into motion at midnight on April 24, 1915, approximately a week after the onset of the siege at Van, the police in Constantinople suddenly converged on the homes of 235 of the city's most prominent Armenian citizens. The bloodshed had begun, and they included leaders of the Ramgavar, Hunchak and Dashnak parties. When the Armenian members of the Turkish parliament protested the midnight raids against the community's Armenian elite, Talaat, writes Sachar, responded thusly: "Your people have come down from the mountains and have occupied Van, with the help of the Armenian population of the city. Now we must take precautionary measures against the Armenians in security areas. Now we shall profit from the favorable situation in which we find ourselves…to disperse your people so that for the next fifty years, no questions about reforms will enter your heads again…"

What great sin had the Armenian defenders at Van perpetrated against Talaat? They volunteered 10,000 of their youths to serve the Ottoman army, they gave generously to the Turkish Red Crescent, and their behavior and loyalty met the standards handed down by Djevdet Bey. Djevdet's latest order was to "turn over 3,000 more men for the military," but the Armenians had learned of the fate that had befallen 200,000 other Armenian volunteers. A fate of death was the order of the day to all Armenians serving the Turkish military. The Armenians refused Djevdet's demand.

Immediately the Turks and their Kurdish collaborators sealed off the entire city. The showdown was about to erupt—the ill-equipped Armenians against the superior enemy. For 30 days and nights the defenders of Van held their ground. On May 16, 1915 the siege ended. Russian troops came to their rescue. In the next two months the survivors of Van made their way to Russian-held Armenia. Those who could not make the journey through the Turkish lines remained in Van. Sachar writes that their faith was death. "The ill and aged who remained in Van were butchered to the last soul when the Turks and Kurds entered. The Armenian quarter was entirely demolished."

In the preface to his book, Sachar addresses today's weakened NATO alliance in that part of the world we know as the Middle East, and states: "It is of more than passing interest, finally, to recall that a vibrant and creative minority race, the Armenians, once shared the heritage of the Middle East civilization; and that, but for the unprecedented tragedy of their genocide (the first of modern times, and now, unaccountably, all but forgotten) the people of Ararat might even today be playing a vital role in the cultural revival of western Asia."

To Howard M. Sachar my everlasting gratitude. When distinguished non-Armenian writers, enriched with their scholarly talents address the forgotten tragedy of Armenia and place it in perspective to the vast American reading audience, they help stoke the flames of justice for the victims of the first genocide in the 20th century.

As we approached Bingol, now a city of mostly Turks and Kurds, I thought of the countless volumes on the genocide of Armenia—including the fresh print from Sachar's powerfully researched account. If thousands of these scholarly researched books were placed in the hands of today's Turkish student, then I could foresee justice developing all across Turkey in a short time. It would be a movement that could topple the cult of denial from government offices in Ankara and the fascist-style Turkish military commanders who boast it is they who decide the fate of Turkey's government.

When we reached our hotel in Bingol, the hour was approaching midnight. Stores and restaurants were closed. The city was asleep. We were tired too. It had been a busy day, and the tempo of activity had taken its toll. Once in my room, I recorded the activities of the day, and quickly fell asleep. In the morning I was chilled knowing that this was the deciding day. This was the most important day of my journey into the interior of the ancestral homeland. It was from Bingol that the airgram reported Parancim had died several years ago in Kutluja—and that it was a meeting of fate with Arousig Mangoian in Moscow that fueled my mission.

Morning came when the filtering rays of daylight pierced through the torn shades of my dingy hotel room. I reached for a cigarette. My heart was beating. The moment of truth was about to unfold on July 24, 1969. All the sorrowing experiences from Merzifon, to Erzurum to Moush now seemed minor. The purpose of my mission was now before me. By the map Nur had left with me, I knew we were only hours away from Kutluja, where Aunt Parancim was last seen alive by Mrs. Topelian on that dark day the Turks set out to destroy the Armenians in the villages of Keghi. Before dressing to join Nur and Mehmet for an early breakfast, I pushed open the windows to my room for some fresh air. I could see the Ingol Mountains, which according to the tourist guide book, closeted numerous iceberg lakes.

Down below in the street, I saw farmers bringing their produce to sell at the market—using ox-driven carts to haul their goods. Later I learned that the poor Kurdish farmers still use the ox-driven carts to get their products to the town market. At breakfast, Nur excitedly said: "Today we find your aunt's grave and your cousins." I shouted back "I still have faith she lives. Don't Muslims have faith?" Nur apologized. He then said "My friend, be thankful she lived a full life. Be thankful she was blessed with children you will meet today. Now you will have an everlasting bond to Turkey.'" For a split second I snapped, shouting I didn't need to bond with Turkey, a nation that massacred my people. I reminded Nur that when my father's forefathers lived in the mountains of Keghi, his forefathers were still living under tents in central Asia. Nur did not respond.

It was now eight o'clock in the morning. Nur suggested we hurry over to the district governor's office where they keep family records to see what they have on Parancim Keteian. As we stepped out of the hotel, I spotted a little handicapped boy at the hotel's entrance. The young boy was selling cigarettes and Turkish candy. I stopped to buy a pack of the popular Samsun tobacco brand. The boy spoke only Turkish. When Nur questioned the youth if "any Ermanie live here," the boy answered: "My grandfather said that many years ago lots of Ermanie people lived here, but during the war they left." When Nur told the boy I was an Ermanie from America, he looked at me, asking "Why did your people leave?" The kind little boy was too young to grasp the answer he sought, so I left it unanswered, but not before thanking him for his interest and wished him good luck at selling more cigarettes and candy. I gave him a shiny Kennedy half-dollar coin as a tip, then we parted.

Within minutes we reached the district governor's office, only to learn he was in Ankara on official business. Then for 40 frustrating minutes, Nur finally found someone in command to help find the family records of Parancim. Soon a mustachioed Turk shuffled into the room we had been told to wait. Nur then showed the man a copy of the U. S. State Department cable which reported Parancim's death had taken place seven years ago...the year of 1962 to be exact. I could recite the message, after having read it a hundred times since it was forwarded to me in January of 1969 by Congressman Lucien Nedzi of Detroit. In part, the cable said: Subject: Welfare whereabouts: Keteian Parancim. Telegram Report From Governor Bingol Province, Eastern Turkey. Identifies Keterine Parancim Perse from Kutluja Village. Keghi District, Bingol Province who died seven years ago. Deceased woman survived by two children, Huseyin and Elif...."

After Nur explained the purpose of our visit, the acting governor spoke of a man named Hakki Yazici, a businessman who was born and raised in Khoops, my father's village. "If any one knows about your aunt, Hakki is the man to see. I will send for Hakki. Now, let me offer you some freshly made coffee until he arrives," the helpful assistant stressed. Some thirty minutes later a small-framed man stepped into the room, asking: "who seeks me. Where is this Ermanie from America. I know the family of Parancim Caglar. I know her children."

I quickly motioned to Nur that he ask some specific questions, and to end the suspense. Did Hakki, a Kurd, know if the woman named Parancim was living or dead. The answer was shattering: "Parancim died in the summer of 1962. She was a noble, beautiful Armenian woman with blue eyes and blondish hair when she was young. Even in her old age she was a beautiful woman, and with a heart of great compassion." I almost blacked out. Nur grabbed me before I slipped off my chair. The room was rolling. Then it stopped. Mehmet helped me to my feet. Then Nur placed his arm on my shoulder. We embraced. But I couldn't stop crying. Where was the justice, I asked. Nur just looked me eye to eye, as he proceeded with more questions, my young Turkish friend also had moist eyes. Mehmet too. Then Nur raised his voice: "My Armenian brother, do not cry. We share the grief you now feel. Do not lose faith. God sent you on a mission. You must now fulfill that mission" Then with his palms reaching out, Nur prayed. "I ask Allah to grant your Aunt Parancim eternal peace in Heaven." After several minutes in the hallway, and now the subject of gawking Turks and Kurds, Hakki urged we leave the building. "I want you to meet the editor of our local newspaper. He is a dear friend and would be honored to meet a journalist from America. Please. Then I will guide you to Kutluja and Khoops.

Hakki's friendship, I learned at the newspaper office, stems from his long admiration for the few Armenians still living in the Keghi district. One of his uncles had married an Armenian woman from Tokat. "My aunt still lives. She is the only Armenian in Khoops. You will meet her. When Nur offered to reimburse Hakki for having left his business to guide us through the Keghi region for the next two days, our new-found friend refused the offer: " I do this to honor our visitor and his father who was born in Khoops. Please, let us travel as brothers."

At the newspaper office, the editor offered us some Turkish coffee and 'katah' which my father used to bake. Katah is dense breakfast bread, made with eggs and butter. Kurds and Armenians in the Keghi district have katah whenever coffee is served.

Emin Mollaoglu, editor of the Bingol Gazette, then chipped in about the pastry bread. "My grandfather said katah was even a favorite of the ancient people of Urartu who used to live on these lands with the Hittites, another ancient race that vanished. Emin was Kurdish and knew his history, even about the Armenians. I marveled at Emin being able to publish a daily newspaper. The type for the four-page paper was all hand-set . Hakki then served notice we should be leaving in an hour to get to Kutluja before sunset That's when the paper's editor said: "We have one Armenian in Bingol. He would be thrilled to meet you. He is a kind, poor man. I try to help him when I can. This Armenian still prays to his Armenian saints."

I agreed. I had to meet Bingol's only known Armenian. My God, only one survivor and the newspaper editor was sending for him. I was sipping on my second cup of Turkish coffee when a haggard, old man in tattered clothes stepped into the paper's office. His face was lined with the wrinkles of age and despair. This weary old man was Hachig Hovanessian—the only Armenian of Bingol.

GIANTS OF THE EARTH

Emin introduced us. "Come Hachig, this young man came from America. He is an Armenian. His father was born in Khoops. Come sit down." Hachig looked at me, with tired but steely eyes that had witnessed the horror of genocide. He spoke in beautiful village Armenian dialect. As he greeted me, Hachig was quick to observe: " You have the blue eyes of the Keghi Armenians. Let me hear you speak. In 10 seconds, the cold steely eyes turned warm and friendly. Hachig was convinced I was an Armenian. At first he thought Emin was playing a cruel hoax. "These Kurds always taunt me. They always say the Turks are the masters of the land and joke with me because I still pray to my Armenian saints. For Hachig, Armenia (Hayastan) still lives, though he's the only Armenian in Bingol.

Hachig was a true giant of the earth. He condemned the Turks in every sentence. He was not intimidated at being the only Armenian. When I cautioned Hachig that the Kurds in the office might know some Armenian, he laughed: "My son. After what I endured even 100 Turks do not scare me. These Kurds tease me, but they also help me."

Hachig's father owned a farm in Hoshkar village before the massacres swept through Bingol district. When I asked Hachig about his family, he told me a story that needs to be told. Here's Hachig's story: "My son, you know I am the only Armenian still living in Bingol. When the Turks started killing our people they left my family alone. My father had one of the largest farms in Hoshkar…but most of the crops were taken by the Turkish military. Then when things got worse my father could not raise enough to satisfy them. Soon the Turks began to confiscate all the Armenian-owned farms in Hoshkar. Then one day they came to our farm. My mother screamed. She told my brothers and sisters to run and hide in the fields. I was the youngest and the only one who did what she ordered. After two nights in the fields, digging up beets and potatoes for food, I was still hungry and scared. I thought it was now safe to go back to my parents. As I entered the front entrance walkway, a Kurdish farmer tried to stop me. But I ran, and got into the farm house. I found them. My father, my mother, my two brothers and two sisters. They were covered with blood. I screamed. The Kurdish farmer dragged me out of the house. He warned "they'll be back, and they'll kill you too." The kind farmer raised me like one of his own sons but he made sure I never forgot what it meant to being Armenian."

The friendly Kurdish farmer buried Hachig's parents, brothers and sisters in the nearby woods. Whenever Hachig got lonely he went to the woods to pray for them. Hachig continued sharing the horrific pain he endured as a child: "As I grew older, my prayers turned to cursing the Turks. I know God forgives me when I curse the animal Turk. I have no one. When the Turks killed my family, they killed all the other Armenians in our village. When I was of age, the older Kurds urged that I become a Muslim and then marry one of their daughters to raise a family. I could not. The Turks killed us because we are Christians. I survived. I did not survive to become a Muslim. I will not surrender my faith in Jesus. When I die I will die as a Christian so I can join my family and Armenian friends in Heaven."

As I looked into Hachig's sunken, tired eyes, I knew this man was the heart and soul of my ancestral country. In all my life I never imagined any one person with the faith and strength I saw in Hachig. Bitterly I held back my tears. I did because Hachig won in his struggle for survival. He never renounced his faith nor Armenian heritage. At age 13 he witnessed crimes against humanity, but never lost faith in God.

When I told Hachig about the Armenians in Soviet Armenia, and in Detroit he was elated. "Good, our people survived." He was especially pleased to know that in Detroit we have four Armenian churches. As we were parting, Hachig asked me what was the name of the church I attended. When I told him, tears ran from the tired eyes of this old man: "Please light a candle for me. When you light the candle, Saint Sarkis will know Hachig has kept his faith and he will welcome me to Heaven."

Before we parted for Kutluja, Emin then thanked me. "In all the years I've known Hachig I've never seen him so spirited as today. You have given an old man a renewed hope. Today Hachig Hovanessian was given new life, and a chance to speak with another Armenian. He looked so peaceful . May God bless you in your mission for visiting with this poor old man."

As Mehmet's dust-covered Chevrolet pulled away from the Bingol Gazette office, I looked back for one final glimpse of Hachig. My heart reached out to this Christian soldier. There he was with head bowed, making the sign of the cross on his tattered jacket. His hands were trembling.

I still have to pray at Aunt Parancim's grave, to let her know she had not been forgotten. But this meeting with Hachig reaffirms my determination to fulfill this mission, and to remind humankind that the Armenian call for justice will never waiver. Men like Hachig Hovanessian stand as a reminder that future generations never forget.

Even now, seven years since our meeting my thoughts for that old man in Bingol remain devout. The story of Hachig is not just another footnote to the Armenian genocide. Hachig is a giant of the earth, like the refugees and orphans of Turkish-held Armenia now building a new altar of freedom in Soviet Armenia.

In closing this chapter it becomes appropriate to refer to John Toland's comments about Hachig's massacred family and fellow Armenians in his penetrating profile of the Nazi executioners in "Adolph Hitler." In the probe into Hitler's fiendish plan of race purity, Toland reminds his readers of the Nazi invasion of Poland and Hitler's intense hate of Jews and the Polish people. In defense of his plan of extermination, Toland quotes the Nazi madman thusly: "It is only in this manner that we can acquire the vital territory which we need. After all, who today remembers the extermination of the Armenians."

Toland's indictment came in 1976, with his new book. For Turkey, there is no escape from the truth. When will Turkey stand trial for its past crimes against humanity?

While Hitler's plan failed, Talaat's worked. It worked because there was no Nuremburg Trial for the Ottoman Turkish government.

CHAPTER TEN

The drive to Kutluja seemed endless. I can not explain the thoughts that flashed through my mind. I would be meeting my Turkish-Armenian cousins. How would I react to having Turkish cousins, a race of people I grew up hating. Did my cousins know their mother was an Armenian? Did they care? Soon I would get the answers.

As Mehmet's car inched up the mountain road, I could see the western tributary of the Euphrates River now shallow and peaceful. Yet in April of 1915 the river was gushing southward, with the bloated bodies of women who had thrown themselves into the river to escape being raped by the Turkish soldiers. But for now it looked peaceful as we came upon the village of Karakocan. Hakki suggested we stop to quench our thirst with the sparkling mountain spring waters. I discovered that the Kurds, like Armenians, like to be hospitable to their guests—and they do with food fit for a king. Soon the table was filled with freshly baked flat lavash bread, thick creamy madzoon(yogurt) smothered with honey. I had not eaten this kind of a spread since my childhood when my mother would make the creamy madzoon with a heavy thick topping called 'sehr.' The friendly villagers were Kurdish. In my travels I do not recall having to exchange heated words with one single Kurd. When told I was an Armenian, the hospitality soared. Except for Nur, most Turks I met were very cool in their reception. That was just fine with me. I could not care one iota about the Turkish people. Their ancestors committed crimes against humanity, and have gotten away without one single penalty. You also should know how the Turks have conned the western world since World War II., when she cleverly remained neutral.

During the Korean War, the Turks sent a brigade to fight alongside the Americans and other United Nations forces to stop North Korea's aggression against South Korea. Ankara has blackmailed Washington ever since, and again during the Cold War Era by allowing American spy planes to fly out of the U.S. air base in Incirlik to monitor Soviet Union activity. The Turks only help when it is to their benefit, and sadly the U.S. State Department has been used as a tool by the Turks to block any attempt by Congress and the White House to brand the massacres of 1915 as genocide.

Now my thoughts were back on what was ahead of us, now at least 30 minutes out of Kutluja. The roadway was a single lane of solid rock. Down below, at least 100 feet, the southerly flow of the Euphrates. I asked Mehmet to stop. I wanted to take pictures of this particular scene. It reminded me of the descriptive testimony taken from the British Bluebook. As I glanced down the steep rocky slopes, I imagined time had gone back to April of 1915, and I could see the corpses of Armenian women and infants floating in the river. My look into the past was broken when Hakki frantically motioned that I step back from the edge of the rocky slope. "Be careful my friend. If you slip and fall, the rocks will tear your body apart before you get to the waters of the Euphrates." I listened and heeded the warning.

Nur then called me back to the car. "Quickly, just down the road is Kutluja. We will be there in minutes. You have reached the final point of your journey." The time had arrived. I was chilled by the fear of what I was going to discover. I recited a prayer to help me face what was waiting for me. Now I could see the village, built along the banks of the Euphrates. The homes appeared to be made of clay and stone. By the time Mehmet brought the car to a full stop, children from the village were upon us. Nur cautioned the excited children to step back. Hakki told the children to fetch the village elders. He repeated: "Tell them we have a visitor from America." Soon the adults were upon us, with curious expressions. As they moved closer my eyes came upon a slender built man. His blue eyes and facial features looked familiar. Then Nur blurted out: "Look, he too has a red moustache like Mr. Kehetian."

Hakki then asked which one of those huddled before us was related to an Armenian woman named Parancim Keteian Caglar. The slender built man who had caught my attention, spoke first. "I am Huseyin, son of Resit and Parancim. What is it you seek." Just to be certain, Nur then asked Huseyin if his mother had any brothers, and if so, did he know them. Huseyin responded: "My mother Parancim said her family died in the great war of 1915, but before the war started two of her brothers went to America. Their names were Dikran and Kaspar." Now we knew for certain, Huseyin was Parancim's son. Even before Huseyin had confirmed his relationship to me, I sensed it.

Now Huseyin was asking questions. When Nur told him that "this man is the son of Kaspar," that I had come from America to honor his mother's family and to fulfill a boyhood pledge to visit Khoops, his father's birth village. Huseyin then stepped forward. We embraced. We did not need an interpreter to express the feeling between two blood cousins. Even now I have difficulty to express my thoughts from that day in my life, July 24, 1969. I only have two first cousins in the world, and now to learn that they're half Turk—the race that I hold responsible for the rape and genocide of the Armenian people. Please, don't lecture me Turkish citizens had nothing to do with the massacres. They sure as all hell knew what was taking place, but shut their eyes—like the German people did years later by closing their eyes while the Nazi goons carried out Hitler's crimes resulting in the massacre of six million Jews.

As the excitement over my arrival began to subside, Huseyin led us to his village home. Within minutes the table in his large living room was overflowing with fresh fruit, flat lavash bread, string cheese, and powdered jelly candy best known in the marketplace as Turkish Delight. Plus we had hot, piping tea on a steamy, hot July day. When the village elders entered Huseyin's home, my Turkish cousin took the floor to deliver a speech, which Nur translated for me: Placing his hand on my shoulder, Huseyin said: "This man is my Ermanie cousin from America. He came thousands of miles to pray at Parancim's grave and to meet her children and grandchildren. My mother always said that one day someone would come to find her here in Kutluja. Now she will rest in peace. The son of her brother Kaspar has made it possible. Thank you Allah."

Huseyin then suggested we go to Parancim's mountain-top gravesite. The sun was setting, and the heat would be less forceful. Nur joined us in the long upward trek. Before we left Huseyin sent an elder messenger to his sister's village. "Tell Elif our cousin from America is here. We will celebrate his visit with a village feast tomorrow. Tell her to bring the children too." Before leaving for the climb to Parancim's mountaintop gravesite, Huseyin suggested I ride on a horse, sensing his cousin from America would have trouble in the climb to the top. I refused. I wanted to walk with him and Nur, and just talk about our families. Nur then repeated: This day is truly the work of Allah. Let us praise Allah."

Several times we stopped to recapture the beautiful scenery as we reached the halfway point to the top, and to let me catch my breath. As we got closer to the top, I could see golden wheat fields from our mountain perch. While the intense heat still prevailed, I felt a chill in recalling Mrs. Topelian's remembrance of the day she last saw Parancim, as the two were trying to escape from the terrorizing Turkish soldiers who had sacked Khoops village. I remember her account vividly, as if I had witnessed the crime. When Parancim fell, the golden wheat fields had turned red with the blood of the Armenians. But now the fields were golden brown, growing and all was quiet. Just the sound of birds and a faint mountain breeze ahead of us. Tucked along the mountain range we could see abandoned homes, most of them crushed by fallen blocks of broken clay and stones. Huseyin said the abandoned village was destroyed by an earthquake many years ago. "I was just a boy then. When the quake hit, chunks of the mountain came crashing on the homes and the village. Many were killed. When our parents rebuilt their village, they wisely constructed it along the banks of the river. The river no longer floods the area in the spring months with the melting of snow. Now if there's a quake we are safe from mountain rocks falling on the people. In the summer months the river gets shallow."

When we reached the top I could see grave stones ahead, with the names of the dead inscribed in Arabic and Turkish. Huseyin then motioned me to join him by a grave decorated with mounds of broken rocks he gathered from the fallen debris at the Kehetian homestead in Khoops...There at my feet, under the clump of rocks rested Parancim Keteian, the sole survivor of Khoops village. Huseyin apologized for not having an attractive gravestone. I assured him Parancim needs no gravestone. God knows those who kept their faith. Before she died Parancim told Huseyin and Elif she wanted them to recite a Christian prayer for her burial. Huseyin said they did with the help of Mariam Bagdasarian who would join us for tomorrow's celebration feast. I fell to my knees to offer a prayer, in Armenian. Huseyin joined me. Removing his cap, and with outstretched hands he chanted a Muslim prayer. As I repeated my Armenian prayer, I cried like a child. My flowing tears dripping on Parancim's clay-baked gravesite. Two years before, on November 26 my father was buried at the Armenian Ararat Cemetery in Fresno, California. Now I knew they were together again, in Heaven. But I was not satisfied, then, or now. We Armenians do not thrive on sympathy for our fallen giants of the earth. As William Saroyan said so accurately, whenever two Armenians meet anywhere in this world, they will create a New Armenia. At Parancim's mountaintop gravesite, overlooking the Euphrates River I swore to avenge the tragedy she endured and the rape and murder of our people. I then realized Soviet Armenia was that New Armenia, and the rule of the Soviets was just another footnote to our history. I knew then that I would return to Yerevan the following year, and express my gratitude to my people for having created a New Armenia out of a state of chaos.

One can not imagine the thoughts flashing through my mind, fueled by my hate and anger of the Turks while I prayed at Aunt Parancim's grave. In the time we were at her grave, I recalled the start of my journey to Merzifon, then on to Sepastia where I visited with heroic Armenians, to my mother's birthplace in Erzurum, with stops at Lake Van, Bitlis, and the district of Moush. While praying at my aunt's grave, my blurred eyes, now swelled by tears, I again pictured Hachig Hovanessian marking the cross of Christ across his heart. I wanted Parancim to know that until my father's last days, he still believed that she had died in 1922 as he had been led to believe. I then crumbled some of the clay from her grave to place into an empty film container. After being on my knees for at least 10 minutes, Nur and Huseyin helped me up. Nur was equally shaken by what he had observed, and said, softly: " I think it is time to join the people in the village. You found your Aunt Parancim, and prayed at her grave. Today she smiles in Heaven."

With one final gesture, I asked Nur and Huseyin to leave me alone at my aunt's grave to share this moment in my life with a woman I never knew, and still do not except to know she was my father's sister. I prayed again, and then could not withhold my anger as I cursed humankind for the suffering my people were forced to absorb. My mission to find my aunt's grave was sparked by a meeting of fate in Moscow just one year earlier. The sun was now setting. For me every July 24 since that day in 1969 now takes on an added meaning and purpose. It was the day I found Parancim and the soul of historical Armenia. I refrained from cursing out of respect at being at my aunt's gravesite. At least she was given a burial site where the dead rest till their souls meet the Creator. But that was not the fate of the more than one million Armenians massacred. For them there were just nameless graves, as the bystanders looked away from the murder of a nation.

Now it was time to bid Aunt Parancim farewell. We didn't talk much in the trek back to the village. I was in no hurry. Again I looked back, now the site was disappearing by shadows from clouds of darkness now moving over the mountains. But for me, even though crushed by the turn of events in this journey, I found my heritage and am ever so thankful to God that I was given life and the heritage of an Armenian.

Before we reached the village I told Nur and Huseyin about our family. I wanted Huseyin to know so he could pass this legacy on to his children. Parancim was one seven children born to Nishan and Hizel Keteian in the village of Khoops. Huseyin then interrupted. He learned about the family tree from his mother. And he had been told that the war claimed the lives of Parancim's sisters Servart and Yeksipert and brother Philibos. Another brother, Takis, died as an infant. Parancim's parents vanished during the war, never to be seen or heard from again. That's the memory Parancim had to live with as a survivor.

Now at the village, the sorrow that had panged at my heart while praying at Aunt Parancim's grave was lessening by the excitement of the children who came to hug and pull at their Ermanie uncle from America. I remember telling Nur: "These kids look like Armenians. Not Turkish." He only smiled. Nur then introduced all of Huseyin's children. He also told me Huseyin's wife, Bedriye, had died the previous summer. Huseyin, only 37, said the love of his children have helped him through the grief of having lost his wife at such a young age. Huseyin's older brother, Mustafa, died several years earlier. Longevity is determined by an individual's person health. If you become ill, whatever the cause, medical treatment is not for poor mountain village folks. But Aunt Parancim was the exception. Huseyin said his mother outlived three husbands. "She was not only an attractive woman, my mother was a healthy, hard-working woman."

The hour was getting late. Hakki said we should drive to Keghi before darkness, and visit Khoops, my father's birthplace, in the morning. But for now, it was time to leave Kutluja, after reassuring we would return for the village feast the following afternoon. We would sleep in Keghi. Hakki said one of his friends in Keghi serves as the town director and has the authority to let us sleep in the empty school dorm, normally used in the summer months by the Turkish military. Before leaving I told Huseyin I still had a lot of questions. We could resume our family talk with Elif during the village feast . I wish I had more time to visit with Huseyin and Elif, but at this point my schedule dictated that we leave for Kharpet after tomorrow's feast. Nur and Mehmet also had commitments back in Ankara.

Hakki's plan for the next 24 hours made sense. We all agreed to avoid any further discussion. Time was too valuable. For me my mission had been achieved at Aunt Parancim's gravesite. Now we had to fill the lost time. We agreed Elif, Huseyin and I could exchange family notes and focus on the unanswered questions. I wanted answers before leaving for Kharpet and Malatya.

Now it's on to Keghi. Darkness was moving in quickly, but Mehmet said we had no cause for worry. With Hakki guiding us, we will get there before total darkness. "My Armenian friend, God brought you to this land of your ancestors. God will protect us, because he knows we are believers in the Almighty." In a change of discussion, I told Mehmet his car was built in my city back in Michigan. The engine of his trusty Chevy had now logged over 150,000 miles. "Most of the time I've driven tourists to our coastal towns in western Turkey. This is the second time I've driven into Anatolia. When you return to your home in Detroit tell the workers who build the Chevrolet cars that this one took you through and over the mountains of your ancestors." Mehmet was a very warm-hearted person. He always referred to driving through the land of my Armenian ancestors. Nur would translate Mehmet's expressions, even the one's focusing on my Armenian heritage. By now Nur and Mehmet were more than my personal tour guides. A bond of friendship was developing. I closed my eyes but for a few minutes when Nur said we had reached Keghi. The best news was Hakki knew the folks at the town coffee shop. It was still open, serving the old men thick Turkish coffee, and sweet pastries—while they competed in the chess game of tavloo. I can not believe it. Here I am in Keghi, on July 24, 1969. Those who can trace their roots to the neighboring villages always identify themselves as being Keghetzees. Hakki saw my excitement at being in Keghi. Nur then stressed that "tomorrow you will drink the water of Khoops, the village your father called as his home and birthplace." Before retiring for the night, I recorded in my journal the motivating activities of the day. Still I was restless, for some 225 miles to the east was Yerevan, Soviet Armenia. By mere chance I turned my transistor radio on, and it was beautiful. Armenian music from Radio Yerevan. Though faint, I could still hear it. Here I was in Keghi, stripped of its Armenian identity and I was excited at being able to pick up Radio Yerevan. I fell asleep.

When morning came, Nur said he could hear the Armenian music, and then caught my attention: "You truly love your Armenian heritage. I also love my Turkish heritage. People who are proud of their heritage are god-fearing people. I am proud you are my friend and brother now. You will be happy when we get to Knoops. Now it was time for breakfast. Hakki found a Kurdish woman to prepare a full breakfast that included string cheese and fresh eggs, hot flat bread, with rich creamy butter and honey. Our stay in Keghi was brief. Just to sleep and a hearty breakfast. I even canceled my earlier plan to scale the Keghi mountains to find the ruins of the Urartu castle. Hakki said it was too risky to attempt even if we had time. While Keghi never made history's headlines, on April 15, 1912 five of its young men were aboard the Titanic in its maiden voyage across the Atlantic Ocean. Only two of the young Keghetzees survived the sinking of the Titanic, after the world's then largest passenger ship struck an iceberg. More than 800 lost their lives. The men were headed for Brantford, Canada. Three years later their beloved Keghi was sacked by the Turks.

Before we left Keghi I told Nur about a new section of Yerevan that's been renamed as New Keghi. Nur was mystified. "How can they take the name of this village and place it in Soviet Armenia? I explained that Armenians in America requested the Soviets rename sections of Yerevan to perpetuate the towns of historical Armenia. Nur remained puzzled: "Your people have a Soviet Armenia now. Why do they still want to claim these lands. These lands belong to Turkey. The Seljuks and Ottomans won it. These lands belong to my people now." I left it at that. This was not the time for another lesson from my British Bluebook.

Before leaving Keghi, a place so dear in the hearts of my Keghetzee friends back home, I knew Ned Apigian and Karl Sogoian would have pitched a tent and send me off, preferring to stay here—the birthplace of their parents. For Ned, an architect and activist in the Armenian National Committee of America, Keghi stands as the "center of the Earth," while Karl, an engineer and frequent contributor to cultural and religious Armenian projects, says repeatedly that having been born with roots to Keghi "was a blessing from Heaven."

Now Keghi stands as a mere shell of its past. I know Ned and Kaloust still visualize Keghi as seen by their parents before the destruction of the homeland. Though my friends represent two generations in age, they share a common Armenian bond. As William Saroyan penned in his tribute to being an Armenian, he was so right is stressing that when two Armenians meet, they seek to build a New Armenia. Ned and Kaloust fit the pattern.

Now it was time for the drive to Khoops. I took one final look at what was left of Keghi, and it was another sad episode. But my spirits were heightened when I spotted towering Mt. Sulbuz—a snow-capped mountain even in the torrid summer season. The ancient Urartu and Hittite peoples worshipped Mt. Sulbuz, and easily understood. She stands as a majestic landmark, an icon if you will, while feeding the western tributary of the Euphrates with her flowing spring waters.

The one person back home who would have treasured my experience at what lies ahead in Khoops is my cousin Steve Khtaian. While our linkage is the Keteian-Postoian clan, Steve is a special person. In many ways Steve is more like a brother. We share the same ideals and political goals for our people, and despise what Turkey represents. We denounce the pro-Turco apologists in Washington who stick their heads in the sand to avoid the truth. What the Turks did to our families in Keghi-Khoops and historical Armenia remains a blot against the world charter of human rights. I know if cousin Steve was here with me he would have planted the tri-color flag of "free Armenia" at the entrances to Keghi. and Khoops.

Yes, when I get to Khoops, I'll get some of the town's treasured soil to take back to Steve.

CHAPTER ELEVEN

As we drove off for Khoops on the morning of July 25, 1969—I still found it difficult to accept the condition of Keghi. From all I have read, and heard from the men and women who had lived in this city before the massacres, the mountain town of Keghi was a central point for the farmers from surrounding villages. The old city also could boast it had a secondary school to prepare its students to attend schools of higher education in Erzurum. But now it was just another mountain town that survived an earthquake several years earlier—and the only new structure was the barracks built to house Turkish troops when on duty to remind the "mountain Turks" who rules the country. I still recall the stories my father shared about Khoops, like the toppled ruins of the Urartu fortress built in the Keghi mountain range. But that morning as we slowly walked to Mehmet's waiting car to take us to Khoops, I recalled reading a concise section about this region in the British Bluebook: "The districts of Erzinjan, Keghi and Baibourt have been devastated by forced emigration. We have no information about the deported people; they say they will be sent to Mosul" in northern Mesopotamia (now Iraq).

Though still saddened by the events of the day in Kutluja at Aunt Parancim's grave, I felt an inner excitement as we drove off for Khoops. As youngsters we promise to pursue an assortment of goals in our adult lives, like I pledged at least several times to my father. I remember the time and place of one such oath. My father had taken me to the U.S. Army's old Fort Wayne Military Reservation, located on the banks of the Detroit River just east of Zug Island. The occasion was the observance of Armistice Day on Nov. 11, 1941. I was all of 11 years old at the time. I remember that special day when I pledged to visit his birthplace when I grew up. I remember the day because a month later Japan pulled its sneak attack of Dec. 7, 1941 on Pearl Harbor. My father served in the U.S. Army during World War I, and often joked that when Kaiser Wilhelm of Germany heard Pvt. Kaspar Kehetian was headed to the war front, Germany agreed to a truce to end the fighting. That's why initially the observance was called Armistice Day. I share this insight into my family tree because it was at Fort Wayne my father first met my mother, Alice Tarpinian, a Red Cross volunteer worker. When I would press my father on why the Turks were able to kill all the Armenians, why didn't our people fight back—as kids do when somebody pushes you in school, Dad told the same story. Like a broken record. "Our people never had a chance to form their own political government let alone to build an army to defend the citizens. When you get older you will learn and understand." I did, and even now I refuse to accept the outcome. What the Turks did to my people must be addressed. I don't care how long it takes.

From what I have witnessed since arriving in Turkish-held Armenia, the enormity of the crime can not be compared to any other global tragedy created by man's inhumanity. What the Turks did took place on the historical lands of the Armenian people, and now we have leaders in Washington who tell me Turkey is an important ally in the Middle East. We should not offend them . That may be true, but so is Israel, but do we turn our backs on the Holocaust victims and meekly bow to militant regimes who want to destroy Israel, who debunk the Holocaust as a myth? No. All the oil in the Middle East can not deter the conscience of America, but Americans of Armenian heritage are told to get off the bus to equality, basic human rights. Sure, some American Armenians might buy that line, but at what cost. To the handful that disagree with me, let me repeat that nearly two million Armenians did not die in the genocide of 1915 so I can tell a co-worker "Gee, I'm glad my parents came to America to live a good life, go to school, and make a lot of money." Yes, they were the refugees, the orphans of a once proud nation. My mother and father never fed me with a silver spoon. They gave me something that I feel blessed with, my Armenian heritage. If

I've annoyed my readers by reliving the genocide page after page, chapter after chapter, I offer no apology. During one of the many debates over recognition of the Armenian genocide, whether the United States should trigger friction with our Turkish ally by enacting such a resolution—Congressman Lucien Nedzi said it the best way possible: "Let us summon truth as our ally...."

God Bless the Detroit congressman and all the others, Democrats and Republicans, who agree truth should be our ally.

After being on the road for an hour, I knew the time was nearing. Soon I would be in Khoops to fulfill another boyhood pledge. When we reached the top of the mountain road, Mehmet had to negotiate a sharp right turn. If he failed, we would have gone over the ledge, and plunge down the steep, slanted mountain side. To make sure we could continue down the rocky road, Mehmet said we should get out of the car for our safety as he tried to get over the rough patch still ahead. As we emerged from the car, I saw Khoops ahead and shrieked with joy. Nur was stunned. "How can you tell that's Khoops?" By now Hakki also repeated my expression. Nur then said "This is truly amazing. It's as if my Armenian brother was returning to his own nest, not that of his father's birthplace." I then explained that the people of Khoops had a picture taken of their village, almost from the same location Mehmet had brought the car to a sudden stop. I had memorized the photo and information my father had shared about Khoops. Like the mountain spring water flowing from back of the altar wall of the Sourp Garabed Church. Huseyin told us the day before that we could find the Kehetian homestead in back of the church, and that he had built a fence, made from stones and fallen tree limbs, in front of where his mother's house stood before the war. We went looking for the fence Huseyin had built, more as a tribute to the past . There was no home now. Just a fence. It was a chilling experience. For Nur too, as he placed his hand on my shoulder: "Look, there is the stone fence Huseyin built. You have found your father's birthplace. Allah will praise this day in your life."

I reached out to push aside the wooden gate, fastened together with twigs and twine. I trembled. On entering the front yard we could see the old tile floor was still in place, though now covered with debris. With a sharp-edged stone I dug away at some of the dirt, and quickly cleared a small patch of the tile floor. Nur then motioned for me to come closer to the fence Huseyin had built. My heart ached. Nur was ecstatic: "Look my brother, wild rhubarb plants in full growth." My father always boasted about the rhubarb his father Nishan grew. He often repeated the rhubarb story when he returned from the Farmer's Eastern Market in Detroit with a batch of the plants. As expected, my father boasted the rhubarb of Khoops was the best in the world." That day in his Khoops I took a taste of the wild rhubarb Nur pulled out of the ground. It was tartly. But it was good. I could not help but to shed a tear of momentary happiness. I then filled another film container with the soil of Khoops taken from the yard of the family home of Nishan and Hizel Postoian-Keteian.

Now we walked over to the ruins of the Sourp Garabed Church. Even Nur was incensed by what we saw and heard. The church was destroyed in 1915, and has been in ruins since then. Here we are in the year 1969 and the desecrated church remains toppled, with no attempts to remove the debris. Nur agreed when I told him that the Turks never expected some Armenian to come back, or for someone like me in search of his heritage to come to Khoops. Like French poet-activist Victor Hugo said, "The Turk has left these lands in ruin." As we poked through the church ruins, Nur spotted a large stone with Armenian writing. The name, chisled neatly, read Mesrop Apkarian. I took a picture of the name-inscribed rock, and on my return to Detroit I learned Mesrop Apkarian was the architect of the church, and the huge rock must have been the cornerstone to the holy site. How chilling. The Armenian graveyards are gone. Nothing with an Armenian inscribed name that we ever came upon, except a building in Moush with the Armenian seminary name still visible. Now we find the architect's name on a church cornerstone in Khoops.

After this experience Hakki suggested we take a break. His Armenian aunt had prepared some Turkish coffee, along with some fresh flat bread and cheese for us to enjoy. Susan Yazici, a widow, was originally from Tokat, a city north of Keghi. Her family had also vanished during the massacres. Speaking in clear Armenian I could fully grasp, she told me she was saved by friendly Kurds in Tokat, then brought to Keghi for her safety. When she turned 16 she was given in marriage to a Kurd—Hakki's uncle. "My son, I had no choice but to obey. I am the only Armenian in Khoops. The Kurds and Hakki's uncle were good to me. It was the Turks who killed my family. You are the first Armenian I've talked to in years," Susan continued. Then this sweet aging genocide survivor told me the rest of the story. While chilling, I remain fully convinced it was guided by fate. Susan said: "Many years ago two Armenian brothers came to Khoops. They said they had gotten permission from the Turkish government to leave the country as repatriates to Soviet Armenia, along with other Turkish Armenians It was after World War II. They came to see their family home before leaving, and wanted to know if any other Armenians were still living here or in Keghi. I told them about Parancim in Kutluja. They knew exactly where their old family home was. It's that big one still standing. The Derderian family owned it." Now it's empty. But still stands.

The two Armenians were the brothers of Arousig Mangoian, the same old woman who told me in Moscow to tell my Uncle Mesrop that her brothers had seen Parancim Keteian before they left Turkey. I took several pictures of the Derderian home Susan Yazici had taken us to see, and on my return home I sent them to Arousig Mangoian, now living with her daughter in Rostov, Russia. This bit of information took me back to the Metropole Hotel in Moscow on the night of July 18, 1968. Before all of this ever transpired, I often questioned those who expressed a devout faith in the Almighty. Now I am a member of the choir. What else could it have been? Sure, coincidence is a reality. I am a newspaperman who believes in the realities of life, not the supernatural. But I feel so much closer to my people now, and the faith that helped sustain their pride during the death marches out of the historical homeland. Before leaving Khoops I excused myself from our group. I needed some time by myself in the ruins of Sourp Garabed. I prayed in memory of the massacred, and I prayed for justice. Khoops is now known as Hupus in Turkish. But the name of the architect of the Armenian Church remains on its cornerstone. It will always be Khoops to its descendants in the Diaspora.

As Mehmet's car began to inch away, for the drive to Kutluja and a village feast in the afternoon with Aunt Parancim's family and friends, I could not erase the cruelties of history. Back on August 1, 1900 the men and women of Khoops drafted a constitution under the name "The Patriotic Union of Keghi-Khoops Village." The intent was clear, the people of Khoops wanted identification within the Ottoman Empire. They were not to be intimidated. Farmers, yes. Village folks, yes. Proud Armenians, yes. My father's village had taken enough crap from the blood-sucking Turks. They did not anticipate what the fucking Turks and Talaat were planning to carry out while Europe was at war. They made the Armenians of Keghi pay the price for adopting a human rights constitution. When the word went out to get rid of the Armenians in 1915, the district village of Keghi—Khoops was high on the hit list in Talaat's black book. But Turkey's Adolph Eichmann paid the price on March 15, 1921 with his assassination on a street corner in Berlin. The bullet that sent Talaat spinning into hell was fired by Soghomon Tehlirian. At his trial, Tehlirian told German authorities he placed his loaded revolver to the bastard's head before pulling the trigger to make sure one bullet did the job on the satanic Talaat. Many years later I got to shake Tehlirian's hand at an Armenian gathering in Boston, and wrote about this national Armenian hero in 1961 while a reporter for the Columbus (Ohio) Citizen-Journal. By the way, a German criminal court jury found Tehlirian innocent on grounds that the assassination was "justifiable homicide."

After the massacres of 1915 the survivors of Khoops amended their Constitution in 1926 to read: "Though our enemies tried to massacre and annihilate our compatriots and so to eradicate the high spirit of patriotism. They failed to extinguish the fire within the hearts of the survivors of Keghi-Khoops Village. Though dispersed to the four corners of the world, our spirit of patriotism is, and will be, immortal."

The group's last general convention was held July 4, 1944 in Detroit. To the fallen giants of Keghi-Khoops, I dedicate this chapter for having stood tall and proud for their human rights. Yes, their spirit of patriotism will be immortal—and will be carried on by their grandchildren until justice is achieved.

Six years after my pilgrimage to Khoops, Ichran Kochyan, secretary of the Keghi-Khoops Patriotic Union, in a June 15, 1970 dated letter requested I speak to his group. He said "We have heard about your trip to our fatherland and your work on slides. We are planning the 70th anniversary of Keghi-Khoops on Sunday, August 23, 1970 with a dinner at the St. Sarkis Church Hall. Most of the guests will be from Khoops, they will be interested to see your work, so dear to them after half a century."

I accepted, and for the next five years I visited Armenian communities in the United States and Canada. But I will never forget my first program for the Khoops gathering in Detroit. My audience, mostly elder survivors of the massacres wept after each color slide of their beloved Khoops was focused on the screen. While my slides of barren Keghi-Khoops restored happy memories of their youth, the tears were for the lost family members in the genocide.

That's why we can not forget the genocide.

CHAPTER TWELVE

Now we were on our way to Kutluja, where Elif and Huseyin would be waiting to celebrate this great day in the ancestral homeland. As we drove southward, we passed through the village of Hogas. We only stopped for water, but soon the villagers were upon us; and again, I found Armenians. These Armenians only knew that their mothers were Armenian. They, as were my cousins, had been raised as Turks. One young man, Ahmet, said his Armenian mother's name was Mariam. "She told me that one of her brothers, Misak, went to America before the Great War and never wrote any letters. Misak lived where they built Ford cars. I think it was Detroit" I promised the young man I would carry his message back to Detroit. On my return I found Ahmet's aunt, and felt good that I had bridged the gap between two other families torn apart by the massacres.

Soon we would be in Kutluja. I was excited again. This time I would meet Elif, Aunt Parancim's only daughter. I also knew that soon after the village feast we would have to leave to reach Malatya and Kharpet by nightfall. I wanted to see these two historic Armenian settlements to complete my journey into historical Armenia—and for having promised my friends back in Detroit that if time permitted, I would visit the birthplaces of their parents. When we reached Elif and Huseyin, they were dressed in their best clothes. They knew I had two cameras and would be taking pictures. Before we even embarked into a discussion, we embraced. The tears of happiness flowed. Elif kept kissing my eyes and forehead, while repeating her mother's name. Nur quickly translated her expressions: "She says you have the blue eyes and facial features of her mother." Once inside Huseyin's home, the village women brought in their freshly prepared foods, from cracked wheat pilaf to chicken and tender chunks of lamb. Then Hakki had a special announcement: "To celebrate this day my Aunt Susan made pagartch for our visitor. When he told her his father used to make pagartch to celebrate special family events, she decided this was one of those special events for all of us. Pagartch is a form of baked wheat bread, scrambled into tiny grains with huge forks, then drenched with hot butter and garlic-flavored madzoon. We Armenians call it the "Feast of the Hittites." Through the centuries pagartch has remained a staple winter meal in the mountains of Keghi since the time of the ancient Hittites. But on this July celebration, it was a special occasion and dictated we have pagartch. I can't express how exciting this was for me. To be eating "pagartch" in Keghi district as my people and the Kurds have since recorded history can not be put in words. I thanked Hakki and asked that he express my deepest gratitude to his Aunt Susan Yazici, now the only Armenian in Khoops. In Detroit the Hardiff Educational Society hosts a pagartch dinner in mid-February every year to raise college scholarship grants for its student members. We always attend. After we consumed a good portion of the prepared foods, now it was time for some freshly brewed Turkish coffee and to ask questions about Parancim, and her life.

Elif and Huseyin proceeded to tell me a story that tore at my heart. Nur also expressed remorse by what we learned. This was their story:

"Our mother said she was a young girl when her two brothers, Dikran and Kaspar went to America. She said her father, Nishan also went to America with another brother, but both came back because the doctors could not help her brother, Philibos, who was losing his eyesight. Soon after they returned, the Great War erupted. There was killing all over the countryside. Then one day Turkish soldiers came to Khoops. They said the older men had guns, and were going to use them against the Ottoman government. Then one of the Turkish soldiers said unless the men surrendered their weapons., they would be arrested. But when the soldiers returned, they started shooting at our village. The elders pleaded to the Turks to stop, but soon both sides were firing at each other. Many were killed. When the shooting stopped. The Turkish soldiers took away the surviving young men. Then we could hear more gun bursts. Then the soldiers came back and ordered all the women and old men to prepare for a journey. We left Khoops with only the clothes we were wearing. Some of the soldiers took away the young girls. Our mothers told us to run. I ran with two of my cousins, but the soldiers caught me when I fell. I was not harmed. A friendly Kurdish family from Khoops paid the soldiers to release me. That's how I was saved. But everyone in my family was killed. I had nightmares for years."

Parancin was the only Keteian to survive the massacre that swept through Khoops. In 1922 she married Yusuf Nergiz, a devout Kurd who knew her family. She lived long enough to marry two Turkish men from Kutluja. Elif continued: "My mother tried to get word to her brothers Dikran and Kaspar that she was alive, but she never heard from them. After she married her first husband, she later heard from an Armenian in Istanbul. His name was Malcolm. He would send her money that he had gotten from his brother Dikran, who was my mother's Armenian sweetheart. His last name was Kostegian. He also went to America, but she never heard from him."

Elif stopped momentarily, after drying her tears she continued to tell a story that still pains me. "This Dikran Kostegian and my mother were promised to each other in marriage. But he never came back. After the killings in Khoops, she began to lose faith she would ever see him again. After she married Yousef she had a picture taken of them together. She then sent this picture to Malcolm in Istanbul to prove she was still alive…and asked that he send it to America. Before my mother died, she told Huseyin and me to get Mariam Bagdasarian to say an Armenian prayer for her at her burial on the top of the mountain cemetery. We kept our word."

Now I had to respond to some of Elif's comments about her mother's life. I explained that brothers Dikran and Kaspar always talked about their sister Parancim, that she was a beautiful Armenian with sky-blue eyes, with hair a yellow blondish color. That they had been led to believe that Parancim died in 1922, according to a man named Malcolm in Istanbul. As for Dikran Kostegian, the man who had been promised in marriage to her mother, I told Elif that he died fighting in the Great

War. Huseyin then asked, where and how was his mother's sweetheart killed. He sat glum as I told him Dikran Kostegian had joined the British army and was killed while fighting the Turks on the Palestine front. He did not ask about Dikran Kostegian again, but I wanted him to know more and proceeded to tell my cousins that their mother's sweetheart wanted to help free Armenia from Turkish rule. As for the breakdown in correspondence, that was truly devastating. When Malcolm in Istanbul would forward checks to Parancim, the bank drafts were drawn on New York banks. She also had gotten some checks from her brother Dikran in America. Parancim knew he was working for the Ford Motor Car Company, but that's where the language translation garbled the message and their lives. When Parancim sent letters to her older brother the envelopes were addressed to Dikran Hateyian. Ford Motor Co. New York City. Her brother worked at the Ford Rouge Plant in Dearborn, and his name had been anglicized to Dick Keteian.

Then Huseyin injected, with tears streaming from his light blue eyes: "My mother thought her brothers had cast her aside because she was married to a Muslim. There were no Armenians left. Her Turkish husband was a good man. He treated her with respect. In total she sent them three letters. One had included the picture with her Turkish husband. But there was no response, except a few times she received money and checks from the Armenian man in Istanbul."

It was then that the puzzle began to fit. There was the letter from Istanbul in 1922 that Parancim was dead. That was the same message my Uncle Mesrop told me when I told him Arousig Mangoian wanted him to know that her two brothers saw Parancim before they repatriated in 1947 to Soviet Armenia. My uncle was so upset over the message from Arousig in Moscow, he repeated, in anguish, "why did I bring him a message from the grave" that was not true. If the elder Armenians in Detroit knew Parancim was alive, but brushed her off as dead because she was married to a Kurd or Turk, it would have been a crushing tragedy. But I will never know. My Uncle Dikran and my father, Kaspar, did not talk to each other throughout my adult life. Each went to their graves never speaking to each other, and did not care to know of each other's fate. Some of the elders said it was just a family feud that grew with time and neither brother was man enough to make amends. Some even suggested that my Uncle Dikran was the man who sent money to Malcolm in Istanbul who would then forward it to Parancim. In Detroit a handful of the still surviving Armenians of Khoops were shocked to learn from me that Perse and Parancim was the same person. Perse was the Turkish name, but my father's sister wanted her children to address her by her Armenian name Parancim. When Malcolm died, the money flow stopped. But my father never knew. All he knew was that the Turks killed his captive sister for a ransom they never got. All the parties to this human tragedy are dead. The Turks were responsible.

The perpetrator of the crimes against my families and my wife's families in the historical Turkish-held Armenian provinces of Keghi, Erzurum and Moush was the Turkish Ottoman government. Any suffering my people still endure, the bastards who committed these crimes against humanity remain free to gloat at carrying out the first genocide of he 20th century

Now it was time to bid farewell to my Turkish cousins, nieces and nephews. I know I will never return to this vast graveyard that was once the Armenian homeland. I've fulfilled my mission in life, and pray that justice will be achieved. If not in my lifetime, it will in the next generation of my family tree.

Before we embraced for the last time, I asked Huseyin and Elif if they could give me a picture of their mother. There was no picture. The only one the family had was sent to Malcolm in Istanbul in 1922 to prove she was still alive. I remain convinced when that picture arrived in America; some of the elders of the Khoops community declared Parancim dead by being the wife of a Turk. In her apology, Elif told Nur to tell me: "I am sorry we have no picture of our mother. But you have your aunt's eyes and facial features. She is now in your heart and she is at rest after you and Huseyin prayed together at her grave yesterday."

As we walked to Mehmet's car, Mariam Bagdasarrian, now in her late sixties, handed me a letter she had comprised about having survived the massacres and to tell the outside world she is still alive. Mariam's Armenian was fluent. She recited an Armenian prayer at Parancim's grave the day my aunt was buried at her mountaintop grave. Poor Mariam, Poor Hachig, Poor Susan, Poor Boghos, Poor Hagop, Poor Parancim. When does it end? It will when justice prevails.

Soon this day will become a series of footnotes in my daily log. Looking back, I saw Elif and Huseyin clutching hands, Mariam just stood with bowed head, praying, and the children jumping up and down for one final look at their departing Ermanie uncle from America. Before too long we had passed through the villages of Temran, Arek, Hardiff and Palu. Our first stop would be Bingol to get Hakki back home, and then we would head for Elazig for an overnight stay before walking through the old Armenian-Byzantine city of Kharpet, where Christian missionaries rescued thousands of starving, orphaned Armenian children from being beaten to death on the march to the steaming hot desert of Der el Zor in Syria.

CHAPTER THIRTEEN

We were near total exhaustion on our arrival in Elazig, took quick hot water baths and hurriedly met for a nice hotel dinner in this growing Turkish town. After stops in Malatya, Kharpet and Kayseri, we would return to modern Ankara for the kind of comfort one does not find in Turkey's eastern Anatolian provinces.

I slept with a heavy heart that night. The last two days in Keghi district had been a painful experience. After a light breakfast Nur returned to tell me that the city's director knew of at least 500 Armenians still living in Elazig and the neighboring villages. I told Nur I was only interested in seeing old Kharpert, once a heavily populated Armenian city—where caravans of Armenian refugees passed through as they were driven toward their deaths in the deserts of Syria and Mesopotamia. As we drove toward old Kharpet, few trees could be seen. Everything appeared dry and barren. Then we could see it, the famed ruins of the Kharpet Castle. Long before the old city's destruction by the Turks, Kharpet boasted a countless number of Greek and Armenian churches—and many shops for travelers. But on July 26, 1969 the approach to Kharpet was but a fading glimpse of the past. Except for a few homes and buildings, the old Armenian section of the city was gone. As if it never existed. But I know it existed. In describing what transpired, the British Bluebook says this of Harpoot's(Kharpet) last days: "At Harpoot, the clearance began on the lst of June, and continued throughout the month. On the 2nd, 3rd, and 4th of July the adjoining town of Mezra was emptied as well. The convoys from these two places and the neighboring villages were terribly thinned by atrocities on the road." But total destruction failed. One church still stands. The Mariam

Ani Church, built right into the mountain rock still serves the 500 or more Armenians in this part of the interior. Though the entrance into the old church was bolted, I could see the inside. No altar. It was bare. We learned from a Kurd that each Easter the Armenians come here to conduct Easter services. But it requires two keys to open the metal bolted door to the church.

Then we found the ruins of the St. Garabed Church. Traveling Armenians passing through here had left signed messages on the charred altar wall of the church. One was signed by Sarkis who asked God's forgiveness. I then wrote my message, in Armenian. It addressed the question of justice. Nur asked what I had written. I told him it was just an Armenian greeting. By now an old Kurd had taken an interest in our presence, as we poked about in the church ruins. After Nur told him about my mission, that I was an Armenian…the Kurd offered to find me some actual pieces of broken church vases from St. Garabed. "If you are a man of faith, you will treasure the broken church vases," he added. The old man then pointed out where the Armenians lived, where they had their schools, where they buried their dead, and where they held summer picnics. How did this old man know so much about the Armenians here? If they were buried here, what happened to their gravestones, I quizzed Nur. The old man responded: "I played in this old Armenian section as a boy. My Armenian friends are gone. Many died in the war, and others were taken away. I live with my memories of those happy days. The gravestones were taken away."

His comment about the missing gravestones reminded me of the train station in Erzurum. Nur expressed the same thought, and did not prod the old man if he knew where the gravestones were taken to, and who removed them. We both knew.

Before we left, the old man took me by the hand. He wanted me to see the ruins of the ancient Harpoot Castle. I visualized the castle in its glorious Byzantine time. It still stands majestically, anchored by a foundation that will probably last for another 100 years unless bulldozed by the Turks because it represents an era free of Turkish tyranny. As I stood with the old man, still hanging onto my hand, it appeared as if all of old Kharpet and its villages of Mezreh and Kisrik had been leveled by a nuclear blast. It was here Arousig Topelian was saved by missionaries and sent to America. When I've talked to Armenian groups, especially those who could claim roots to Kharpet, they cringed at the color slides of the birthplace of their parents. It was barren and leveled of life—not by a nuclear blast, but destroyed by the Ottoman Turks. Turks say it never happened.

In a penetrating look at "Genocide—Its Political Use in the Twentieth Century," scholar Leo Kuper wrote in 1981 that "the Armenian genocide is the forgotten genocide of the twentieth century, remembered mainly by Armenians." The professor's scholarly-researched work on genocide, while addressing the Armenian genocide, also weighs into the genocides of the Jews, the Bangladeshis, and the Hutu. As a professor emeritus at UCLA, Kuper's work on "how to write on the theme of genocide and how to convey it in a comparative study" is etched together with scholarly documentation—and is must reading by students of history and American politicians who are captivated by the dancing of whirling dervish Turkish lobbyists.

After leaving Kharpet, it was a matter of time we would pass through Malayta, then on to Kayseri for our last night in eastern Turkey. Our stay in pillaged Turkish-held Armenia was just over a full week. I could not take much more without losing my control. Malatya's history goes back to the ancient Hittites, nearly 3,500 years ago. Even then it was known as Malatya. My friend Paul Kulhanjian, the Detroit public school educator, always reminded me about the courage and wisdom of the Armenians of Malatya. But time did not permit an overnight stay. If it did I would have wanted to drive southward to the plains of Adiyaman and Mount Nemrut—where the extinct Comagenes people ruled and built towering temples dedicated to Zeus and Apollo. For the Turk this ancient past has no connection to the Turk, and they fully know it. The first Turk to set foot in Asia Minor did not come until the turn of the 10th century.

When we reached Kayseri the hour was close to eight o'clock in the evening. The city has a lasting link to ancient Greece, since historians had referred to the city as the Athens of Asia Minor. For Armenians, Kayseri was also deep-rooted, with at least 1,000 still living here and serviced by

St. Gregory the Illuminator Church. We had a lavish dinner on the rooftop restaurant of our hotel. Nur agreed we should call on the church in the morning before our final drive to Ankara. After breakfast we found the church, but unfortunately its pastor, the Rev. Fr. Krikor Mardirossian, had left for Turkey's interior two days earlier to conduct an Armenian wedding ceremony in Bitlis. The old church was built in 1885 and somehow escaped the ravages of Turkish rule and the carnage of 1915. This particular day was Sunday, July 27. Before we left the beautiful church, two young Armenians appeared. Mihran and Sarkis had heard of my arrival, and rushed over to St. Gregory. Meeting them was refreshing. Both young Armenians spoke glowingly of their heritage and expressed great pride at their ability to speak fluent Armenian. My two young Armenian friends said they conduct annual visits into the interior to encourage young Armenians to come to Istanbul where they can retain their Christian faith and heritage.

I felt good after meeting Mihran and Sarkis and marveled at their courage to stand up as two proud Armenians in a sea of Turks. For Nur this was another learning lesson on how Armenians seek each other and are bonded by our culture and a heritage the Turks could not eradicate through genocide.

Mihran and Sarkis also praised Armenian Americans for helping Armenians in Istanbul and the Diaspora, in particular Detroit industrialist Alex Manoogian, revered as the pillar of strength that guides the worldwide AGBU, Armenian General Benevolent Union. "When Armenians reach out to help us, the Turks leave us alone to operate our schools and churches. We are indebted to the AGBU and Mr. Manoogian." My two young Armenian friends were also pleased when I told them that even with his wealth and distinguished role in American life, Mr. Manoogian remains a humble man who places his Armenian heritage at the highest level. The hour had now arrived for our drive to Ankara. We shook hands, and in true Armenian fashion, we embraced.

On leaving Kayseri, I knew my journey to historical Armenia was about to end. By nightfall we were in Ankara, the capital of Turkey. Though I have no love for the Turks and their nation, I had to confess that it was good to be in Ankara after having spent what seemed like a lifetime in barren, historical Armenia. The following morning at the Turkish tourist office, we were informed the next flight for London would not be until Thursday. After several phone calls I was successful at making arrangements to leave Ankara on Tuesday for an early morning flight to Istanbul—then on to Rome for an overnight stay. With Monday free, Nur suggested we visit the tomb of Ataturk, the founder of so-called modern Turkey. I was in no mood to pay homage to the bastard who in 1920 ordered the attack on the independent Armenian republic of 1918, but was denied the chance to finish what Talaat had sought to accomplish. The Soviet Red Army moved into Yerevan to put an end to the Turkish advance. But out of respect to Nur, I agreed to visit the Ataturk Memorial. On our way to the national shrine in downtown Ankara, Nur sounded what appeared to be an alert. "Be careful with your film at the airports in Ankara and Istanbul. I agreed to carry the film in my carrying bag and place the two cameras in my suitcase with a few rolls of exposed film as a decoy if the Turkish customs agents try to confiscate my rolls of film that captured what's left of historical Armenia.

On reaching the Ataturk monument, we walked through an impressive approach to the tomb, flanked by stone-carved lions. At midpoint, I asked Nur why the architects of the memorial for Ataturk had placed replicas of the mountain lions of the Hittite Era to guard the pathway to the great Ataturk. I again pressed my friend. Nur you know the Hittites ruled this region in ancient times, and fought the Mamelukes of Egypt. The Turks did not come to this region until the 10th century. I knew I had pushed my young Turkish friend a bit too far. Nur kicked his heels in disgust. He fumed: "My roots came from central Asia. I am proud of that fact. I am a proud Turk like you are a proud Armenian. We are brothers now."

I tried to settle my friend, assuring him that where people come from is not the issue. The issue is how we treat each other and other citizens of the world. In all the Turkish tour books I had been able to gather, the only mention of Armenia was the Armenian Church in Kayseri that I had visited on my last day in the interior. Not one iota that a nation of

Armenians lived here. If they did then questions would be raised, and not the kind the Turks want to be pressed at having to respond.

After spending a good portion of the day with Nur and Mehmet, we returned to the hotel in time for dinner—and a farewell toast that brought a Kurd, a Turk and an Armenian together. While it was fate that brought me to Turkish-held Armenia I doubt if I could have accomplished my mission without the help of Nur and Mehmet. We then embraced for our final farewell.

But it was not our final farewell. When I got up early the following morning to have breakfast and catch a cab to the airport, Nur and Mehmet were in the lobby. Nur greeted me: "Our Armenian brother, we decided to make sure you did not encounter any problems. We will take you to the airport. When you get to your home in America, write us that you are safe." I promised, and said I would send pictures of our journey "into Anatolia."

When I boarded my Turkish Airlines flight for Istanbul, I looked back and saw tears of happiness trickle from the eyes of my friends. I will remember Mehmet Unlu and Nur Tanisik forever. They helped me fulfill a mission in search of the heart and soul of Armenia, and with their help and compassion I found it at a gravesite overlooking the Euphrates River—and in Erzurum, Keghi-Khoops and Moush.

My two friends are proud of their Kurdish and Turkish heritage. I seriously doubt if Nur will ever acknowledge the sins of Turkey's past. If he does in his later life, it will only come when other educated Turks join ranks to demand that their government admits to the genocide of 1915—and agrees to negotiate the return of land seized illegally after the genocide of Turkish-held Armenia.

Some of my colleagues say I'm a wishful dreamer. Yet I remind the doubters that the corrupt, dictatorial Soviet Union collapsed in 1991 without a nuclear showdown between the United States and the Kremlin. I have faith justice will come to the Armenian nation.

After the short flight to Istanbul, I learned my Alitalia flight to Rome would leave as scheduled. I had a two-hour wait. I could not sit and remain calm. I also knew I should not wander away from the departing gate or I might provoke some questioning about my lack of patience.

I was still afraid that at the last moment, Turkish security would confiscate my rolls of film. Then there was a light of hope. I saw a string of Catholic clergymen sitting on one of the bench seats, at least a dozen. They had the physical appearance of being ethnic Italians, except one who looked like an Armenian Catholic priest I knew in Detroit, the pastor of St. Vartan Armenian Catholic Church. As I approached the familiar churchman, he also smiled. I was right. He was the Very Rev. Joseph Kalajian. Fr. Kalajian was waiting to board the same flight to Rome. "This is beautiful. We will sit next to each other and talk about our trips while on the flight to Rome," my church friend repeated.

When the boarding announcement was sounded, I walked at Father Kalajian's side. Once aboard the plane I relaxed. I was aboard an Italian airliner and free of Turkish authorities. After explaining to the good father the purpose of my journey, his story was similar. Fr. Kalajian had joined a group of his Vatican clergy brothers for a tour of southern Turkey, but with a primary mission to visit a village in the Adana province where he was born. Before he shared his harrowing story we each ordered a glass of red wine to toast our meeting in Istanbul. The good father knew my parents, and said "your sister Isabel had a beautiful voice. She honored our church several times by singing at St. Vartan cultural programs." After a lifetime at serving the Catholic church, my friend returned to his birthplace in old Cilicia Armenia, once ruled by King Levon until the fall of Cilicia Armenia to the Mamelukes of Egypt in 1375 A.D. Father Kalajian's story is but another footnote to the genocide.: "When the Turks struck our village, they took my father away and killed him. Then they forced the remaining village people, mostly old men, mothers and their children to get ready for the march to Syria. Before our caravan left, my mother had taken ill. She died and was buried in Keferdez with other Armenians who had died from diseases and Turkish brutality. I was just a boy of about 10 years old when the march started. My father's friends tried to help me. They gave me bread and water. But soon the water and bread was gone. About one third of the caravan made it to Syria. We reached the desert of Der el Zor. You could smell the stench of rotting bodies of Armenians. I collapsed from hunger and exhaustion. I was sick and thought I would die like all the other Armenians. But a kind Syrian woman fed me and treated the burns and blisters on my face and feet. She then turned me over to Catholic missionaries in Aleppo. I thought I was in Heaven. The missionaries placed me in an orphanage until I recovered. From that day I pledged to God to serve the church until my last breath of life. That's why I returned to the village of my birthplace in Cilicia Armenia to pray for my mother and father. I have not forgotten them. Never did, never will."

I had to wipe my tears. So did the good father, as he apologized for breaking down. This was a story he only shared with the clergy while on the path to priesthood. As our aircraft circled Rome, Fr. Kalajian suggested I stay for a few days to meet with his fellow Armenian Catholic priests, and visit Rome. I explained my flight plans were locked in and could not change them. I would have to catch a morning flight to New York, and ultimately return to Detroit. Before we landed, Fr. Kalajian repeated: "We must not lose faith. God has not forgotten our suffering. Our reward is survival. We Armenians have survived. The Turk has yet to meet his fate, and when he does—God will punish him for the crimes against our people. We must carry the cause for justice. We are Christians. We must not lose faith."

Oh how I wanted to curse the bastard Turks after forcing the good father to recall the death march he survived, while losing his entire family. But I with-held the use of foul language while cursing the Turks. My friend is a devout religious leader. Even as he described the torture he had endured Fr. Kalajian spoke with compassion. He only seeks justice. He is truly a giant of the earth.

My journey to the land of my people, while disheartening in Turkish-held Armenia remains alive in present-day Soviet Armenia. I will return to Yerevan next year. I must. Communism is but another chapter in the lives of the Armenian people. Our people will grow and prosper, and hopefully in time the ideologies that pit communism versus capitalism will find the pathway to co-exist and to respect each other's platform of life. What I have seen and encountered in historical Armenia has been a nightmare. It all started at my meeting of fate with an old woman in Moscow. It was her chilling message that ultimately took me to a mountaintop grave overlooking the Euphrates in historical Turkish-held Armenia.

The Turkish plan to destroy the Armenian race failed. It failed because the refugees and orphans of Van, Bitlis, Moush, Erzurum, Sassoun, Keghi, Sepastia, Malatya, Kharpct and Erzinjan survived as the true giants of the earth to build a "New Armenia" in present-day Soviet Armenia. As William Saroyan penned: "...go-ahead, destroy Armenia, burn their homes and churches then see if they will not laugh, sing and pray again for when two of them meet anywhere in the world, see if they will not create a New Armenia."

Father Kalajian was right. "We must not lose faith. We have survived."

EPILOGUE TO GIANTS OF THE EARTH

Years after my journey into historical Turkish-held Armenia, I can still see a weary Hachig Hovanessian who thought he was the only Armenian survivor of the Turkish massacres in Bingol Province, and asked that I pray for him at my church in Detroit—while a lonely Mariam Bagdasarian sketched a letter for the outside world to know that "Mariam is still alive."

Hachig and Mariam were in their late sixties when we parted. Even now I pray for them, knowing that these two "giants of the earth" are now in Heaven.

For Aunt Parancim, I shall never forget the time I spent at her gravesite. Her children now know my father went to his grave still grieving about his lost sister. I remain convinced, even now, that it was God's hand that guided me to Aunt Parancim's mountaintop grave to fulfill my mission. Though Aunt Parancim's family had no picture of their mother to share with me, I felt her presence in my heart while I prayed at her grave.

In my 50 years as a journalist in Detroit and Columbus, Ohio, I never hesitated at expressing pride in my Armenian heritage while pursuing a career at protecting the public's right to know. I can point out that as a journalist I also earned the respect of my colleagues, as evidenced by serving as president of the Detroit Press Club, the Society of Professional Journalists—and then in 2006 to be honored with a "lifetime achievement award" by the Journalism Department of Wayne State University.

When pressed by my media friends about the Armenian Genocide, and why is it so critical that Turkey admit to the crimes committed by the old corrupt Ottoman Turkish government, I can only repeat what I have said, lectured and expressed for countless times in editorial comments in newspapers I have reported for and managed as an editor. How can I forgive present-day Turks when they deny the genocide and massacres that violated my ancestors?

Turkey says there was no genocide, that they merely dispatched the Armenians from the interior to the deserts for their own protection and to quell civil disturbances. Hitler used the same technique by sending Europe's Jews to concentration camps where the Nazi executioners carried out their heinous crimes.

In its April 24, 1985 editorial "Remembering the Armenian Genocide," The Detroit News said when Hitler began to slaughter the Jews, he was warned that the world would not tolerate such atrocity. To which he replied, "Who today remembers the Armenians."

While calling for the recognition of "the Armenian Genocide" in its October 24, 2000 editorial, the Detroit Free Press said "It's not ancient history. Unless we acknowledge and learn from it, we can never prevent it from happening again."

Clearly, there can be no time limit at correcting an injustice against humanity. To this very day the Turkish government denies it was genocide, and rebuffs talk of wholesale massacres. Instead Ankara says the 1915 relocation of the Armenians to the deserts of the Ottoman Empire was to quell threats of a civil uprising at its border with Russian-controlled Armenia. It is in Turkey's best interest to correct the human tragedy the Ottoman government executed in 1915-23, first by condemning its past leaders and then seek to resolve its territorial resolution with Armenia. A vibrant Armenia, along with an equally vibrant Turkey free of its past crimes against humanity can stand as examples at the spreading of civil and economic freedoms throughout the troubled Middle East.

During my eight days in Turkish-held Armenia, I could not find a trace of my historical roots. Nothing was left but the crumbled ruins of Armenian homes and churches. I've been asked if I plan to return to the historical Armenian districts. I have to be blunt in my response. I have no desire to relive what I endured in 1969. If Turkey acknowledges genocide was carried out against the Armenians, and is willing to negotiate the return of portions of Wilson Armenia and the 1918 Armenian Republic, then yes, I would be on a plane bound for Turkey. I would bow again at Aunt Parancim's grave to tell her that our people have achieved justice for the victims of the Armenian Genocide, and have regained tracts of historic Turkish-held Armenia.

That's why it is critical that Turkey recognize the sins of her past, sins that claimed the lives of 1.5 million Armenians, drove thousands off their historical lands into the deserts, and turned former Soviet Armenia into a nation of refugees and orphans. She refuses to admit to the genocide to protect Turkey's sinister past and fear of punishment to fit the crime.

For the Armenian people, Turkey's punishment means the return of depopulated Armenian lands seized after the genocide crime of 1915-23. The Armenian Genocide was plotted and executed to remove the call for reform and statehood. Talaat's plan worked. Now Turkey must face the punishment of its past government by returning the barren lands it seized by executing the genocide.

But the Turks say Mustafa Kemal Ataturk's founding of the Turkish Republic in 1923 had nothing to do with the Ottoman Turkish Empire, so why condemn present-day Turkey. When the gangsters of Hitler's Nazi-ruled Germany were tried and convicted for their crimes against the Jewish people, the Democratic Republic of Germany also denounced the Nazi leaders of Germany, and sought the forgiveness of the surviving Jews and citizens of the civilized world—and still does to this very day. By denying the massacres and genocide carried out against the Armenian people, present-day Turkey remains linked to that crime against humanity. The Turks must acknowledge the genocide of 1915-23 if they want to rid their nation of the festering cancer that continues to haunt its past.

For the Armenian people their greatest battles for freedom were fought May 23-28, 1918 at Sardarabad, Bash Aparan and Karakilisse when they repulsed the advancing Turkish army seeking to finish the Ottoman government's plan of genocide. In one of my pilgrimages to the Sardarabad Memorial, I found myself surrounded by children from the historic town of Sardarabad. It was exciting. The genocide failed. My people survived 600 years of Seljuk and Ottoman Turkish rule, saw their 1918 free republic fall in 1920 to a joint Turkish-Soviet attack, then survive 70 years under the rule of Soviet communism—until 1991 when the Kremlin collapsed and Armenia was free again.

This memoir I share with you is not a history of Armenia, but snapshots of what I've read, experienced and witnessed in my search for Aunt Parancim and my Armenian roots. While the thrust of what I have shared in "Giants of the Earth" focused on the pain and agony of the Armenian people, there is still room to celebrate its very existence when reviewing the course of history. When one looks at the tragedy of Armenia, then they have every right to question its very durability in the 21st century.

In the 2009 Index of Economic Freedom, the Wall Street Journal and The Heritage Foundation placed Armenia with a ranking of 31st out of 179 ranked nations—proving freedom is still the winning formula. Turkey was given a ranking of 75th. How ironic that little Armenia, now free again after having endured the 1915 genocide, its people stripped from their ancestral homeland in Turkish-held Armenia, and forced to live for 70 years under the heel of Soviet communism, was still able to survive as a people who adhere to the credo that economic freedom is still the winning formula—and ranked ahead of Turkey which still struggles in its state of denial.

In dedicating this memoir to the people of present-day Armenia, and my cousin, the late Rev. Vartan Kassabian, I urge fellow Armenians across the globe to visit Yerevan to absorb the spirit of a "New Armenia" that stands in the shadows of Biblical Mt. Ararat.

You ask who the people of present-day Armenia are. They are the descendants of the refugees and orphans from the Armenian districts of Turkish-held Armenia.

William Saroyan said it the best: "...when two of them meet any place in the world, see if they will not create a New Armenia."

That's why I call my people the "Giants of the Earth."

Manufactured By: RR Donnelley
Momence, IL USA
February, 2011